AnimalWays

Lizards

AnimalWays

Lizards

Dan Greenberg

Benchmark Books

MARSHALL CAVENDISH
NEW YORK

With thanks to Dr. Dan Wharton, director of the
Central Park Wildlife Center, Wildlife Conservation Society,
for his expert reading of this manuscript.

Benchmark Books
Marshall Cavendish
99 White Plains Road
Tarrytown, NY 10591-9001
Website: www.marshallcavendish.us

Library of Congress Cataloging-in-Publication Data
Greenberg, Daniel A.
Lizards / by Daniel A. Greenberg
p. cm. — (Animal ways)
Includes bibliographical references and index.
Contents: All shapes and sizes—What is a lizard?—The lizard body—Lizards in action—
Getting to know lizards—Reproduction—Lizards today and tomorrow.
ISBN 0-7614-1580-7
1. Lizards—Juvenile literature. [1. Lizards.] I. Title. II. Series.
QL666.L2G736   2003   597.95—dc21   2003002566

Photo Research by Candlepants Incorporated

Front Cover Photo: Stephen Dalton/Photo Researchers Inc.

The photographs in this book are used by permission and through the courtesy of:
Animals/Animals: Zig Leszczynski, 2–3, 13, 19, 29 (top), 37, 53, 89, 97; Peter Weimann, 9;
James H. Robinson, 10; Allen Blake Sheldon, 12; Austin J. Stevens, 27, 33, 88; Mella
Panzella, 29 (lower); Paul Freed, 38, 59, back cover; Joe McDonald, 40; Marian Bacon,
41; Gerard Lacz, 46, 67; George H. Huey, 55; Jim Mantis Frazier/OSF, 57; 46; Raymond A.
Mendez, 64; Joyce & Frank Burek, 69; Mark Jones, 72; Doug Wechsler, 75; Robert A.
Lubeck, 77, 94; James H. Robinson, 83, 85; HeinrichVan Den/ABPL, 93; Keren Su, 99.
Photo Researchers Inc. : Art Wolfe, 11; E.R. Degginger, 14; Nuridsany et Perennou, 22;
Jany Sauvanet, 31 (left); Michael McCoy, 31 (right); A. Cosmos Blank, 51; Barbara
Strnadova, 52; R. Van Nostrand, 70; Tom McHugh, 73; G. C. Kelly, 81; M. H. Sharp, 86;
Suzanne L. Collins, 91; Herbert Schwind/Okapia, 103; *Reunion des Musee' Nationaux/Art
Resource, NY*: 15. *American Museum of Natural History/D. Finnin*: 23 (#2A23710).

Printed in China

3 5 6 4 2

Contents

Animal Kingdom

CNIDARIANS

coral

ARTHROPODS
(animals with jointed limbs and external skeleton)

MOLLUSKS

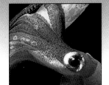

squid

CRUSTACEANS

crab

ARACHNIDS

spider

INSECTS

grasshopper

MYRIAPODS

centipede

CARNIVORES

lion

SEA MAMMALS

whale

PRIMATES

orangutan

HERBIVORES
(5 orders)

elephant

ANNELIDS

earthworm

CHORDATES
(animals with
a dorsal
nerve chord)

ECHINODERMS

starfish

PHYLA

VERTEBRATES
(animals with a
backbone)

SUB
PHYLA

FISH

fish

BIRDS

gull

MAMMALS

AMPHIBIANS

frog

REPTILES

LIZARD

CLASSES

RODENTS

squirrel

INSECTIVORES

mole

MARSUPIALS

koala

SMALL MAMMALS
(several orders)

bat

ORDERS

1 All Sizes and Shapes

They are here, there, and everywhere. On fences, along walls, under rocks, inside bushes, in almost every habitat and climate on Earth, lizards dart and dash, creep and crawl, squirm and wriggle. Lizards are the biggest group in the reptile class, numbering some 3,000 or more species.

Like snakes, their close cousins, some lizards go by names that make them sound pretty horrifying: dragon, monster, and bloodsucker, not to mention giant, horned toad, jungle runner, and thorny devil. A few lizards are in fact extremely nasty customers. The Gila monster of Mexico and Arizona, for example, has a poisonous bite that can put the life of a human being in serious jeopardy. The horned toad, on the other hand, does not bite when it gets mad, it squirts blood—out of its eyeballs—directly at the enemy! Finally, the Komodo dragon frightens its enemies the old-fashioned way—simply by being, well, a dragon! What else would you call a lizard that is almost as long as a compact car and eats deer, wild boar, and the occasional human?

LIZARDS SUCH AS THESE GREEN IGUANAS MAY SEEM LIKE MINIATURE DINOSAURS, BUT THEY ARE ACTUALLY MORE CLOSELY RELATED TO SNAKES.

But in actuality, instances of lizards being menacing or brutal are few and far between. Though some lizards may look like miniature dinosaurs or modern-day dragons, most are decidedly unferocious and harmless. While a handful of lizard species are known to be aggressive and even dangerous, most are shy and secretive, and quite a few are considered cute, friendly, playful, and ideal as beloved household pets.

Why are lizards so appealing to people? In part, because they are quick and elusive, colorful, unthreatening, and small. Most measure 1 foot (30 cm) or less in length. Less common, but still quite numerous, are the medium-sized lizards, such as the 14-inch (35-cm) eastern collared lizard, *Crotaphytus collaris*, or

THE CHUCKWALLA IS A MASTER OF SQUEEZING BETWEEN ROCKS. A PREDATOR MAY GET A CHUCKWALLA IN ITS GRASP, BUT IT WILL NOT BE ABLE TO PRY IT OUT OF THE ROCKS.

THE UNDISPUTED KING OF ALL LIZARDS IS THE KOMODO DRAGON, WHICH LOOKS LIKE A THROWBACK TO SOME PREHISTORIC TIME.

the chuckwalla, which is usually smaller than the 16- to 18-inch (40- to 45-cm) *Sauromalus obesus*. Rarer still are the jumbo species, such as the green iguana, *Iguana iguana*, which is usually almost 6.5 feet (2 m), or the legendary super-jumbo Komodo dragon, *Varanus komodoensis*, which, though usually not quite that large, occasionally tops out at 10.3 feet (3 m) in length, and again in unusual cases, weighs up to 330 pounds (150 kg).

No matter what their size, virtually all lizards seem to be darting and elusive, although the top running speed of most species is often a bit overrated. Lab experiments show that a typical lizard, such as the six-lined race runner, *Cnemidophorus sexlineatus*,

runs at only about 15 to 20 miles per hour (24–32 kmh). While this may not seem exceptionally fast, even the swiftest human would find it impossible to catch up to one of these critters when it is skittering along the ground.

Color is a defining characteristic of lizards. Their color is used mainly for reproductive identification. Their colorful bodies reveal an interesting fact about lizards: Vision is their primary sense. (That isn't true of many of their reptile relatives.) Lizards use their vision to hunt prey, avoid predators, find and identify mates, and stake out territory. Some lizards, like the chuckwalla or many nocturnal geckos, are quite dull in color. Most females are colored in modest grays, dull tans, or neutral browns or greens. But the males of many lizard species, such as the emerald swift, *Sceloporus malachiticus*, the fire skink, *Lygosama fernandi*, or the breathtakingly spectacular panther chameleon, *Furcifer pardalis*, are brightly colored.

Of course, an animal that loudly advertises its existence in bold oranges, reds, and yellows may be asking for an early death. Lizard predators, including birds, snakes (a number of which specialize in lizards as food), and mammals are attracted to color. In fact, some lizards do get snapped up because of their flamboyance. But for the most part, color is something that lizards try to conceal, hiding it on the underside of their bodies. If an attractive female happens by, then the male struts its stuff—

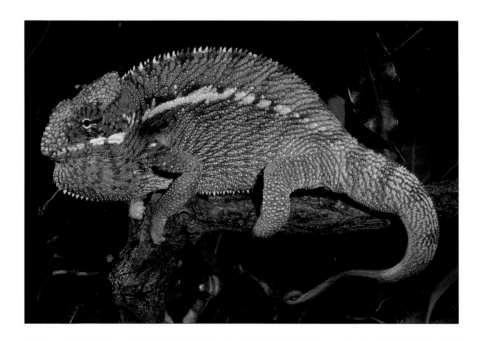

SOME OF THE MOST BEAUTIFUL—AND BIZARRE—LIZARDS ARE THE CHAMELEONS. THESE PANTHER CHAMELEONS ARE SHOWING OFF THEIR BRIGHT COLORS.

lifting its legs and flashing its blazing belly for the female to appreciate. If, on the other hand, an enemy is nearby, the male keeps its belly—and its fiery colors—low to the ground and out of sight.

The third trait characterizing most lizards is their nonthreatening nature. The only other nonthreatening reptiles are members of the turtle family. In folklore and mythology, lizards generally

THE IGUANA IS
ONE OF THE FEW
LIZARD SPECIES
THAT IS HUNTED
BY HUMANS
FOR FOOD.

also have a favorable image. While some Western sources regard lizardlike dragons as gruesome and evil, most Eastern and Middle Eastern cultures see lizards as good. The Chinese, for example, traditionally see dragons as friendly creatures that bring nobility, good fortune, and wealth.

In many Asian cultures, geckos especially are thought to bring luck. Newlyweds are said to listen for the call of a gecko on the night of their marriage to bring their union prosperity and good fortune. The ancient Europeans and Greeks saw lizards as symbols of hopefulness and wisdom. The Romans viewed lizards as symbols of rebirth.

Many myths and folktales feature prominent lizard characters. The lizard king Mo'o appears in the myths of Hawaii and several other Polynesian cultures, while in Amazon myths the lizard is the lord of animals. Two especially interesting lizard myths come from Africa and Australia. The African Bantu tell of a chameleon who was sent by the god Unkulunkulu to tell the human race that its members would live forever. Unfortunately, the chameleon was delayed and a second lizard was sent bearing the message that the days of people were going to end. In

WHILE EUROPEAN CULTURES SAW DRAGONS AS HORRIBLE ENEMIES, THE CHINESE VIEWED THE DRAGON AS A NOBLE CREATURE THAT BROUGHT GOOD LUCK AND HEALTH.

Australian myths the lizard god Tarrotarro is given credit for splitting the human race into males and females, and giving people the gift of artistic expression.

Europeans may have viewed lizards unfavorably because they are not usually found in cold or temperate climates. Since people are likely to regard the unfamiliar with suspicion, middle and northern Europeans viewed the rarely seen lizards as evil creatures.

In tropical locations, on the other hand, lizards play a much more prominent role in everyday life. In the West Indies, the anole lizards are as much a part of daily existence as squirrels are in Boston or Kansas City. Scampering on and under every tree and branch, these bright creatures are a familiar part of the landscape, and they are no more likely to be feared than, say, rabbits in a more temperate part of the world.

Similarly, in many tropical locations lizards are a key part of the indoor environment. Like fully alive room decorations, geckos hang on the walls of even the most civilized homes and public buildings in these climates. Why are these trespassing

Anole Lizard

intruders tolerated? Because they are not intruders at all, but invited guests who are welcomed even into the finest homes to do their job—catching insects. Instead of being horrified at the sight of an animal running loose, people feel reassured by the presence of a gecko. A gecko in the house means one thing: housefly and cockroach populations will be kept to an absolute minimum.

What else is there to know about lizards? In the chapters that follow, some impressive and amazing feats of lizards will be presented. Lizards that fly through the air, swim on land, and walk on water. Sound impossible? Well, that describes the flying dragon, which can soar through the air; the sand fish, which can "swim" through sediment the way a fish swims through water; and the brown basilisk, which, instead of swimming through water, runs along its surface.

Lizards also have amazing physical characteristics. There are lizards that have three "eyes," lizards that have up to one pupil that closes into four tiny holes, and lizards whose eyes can look in two different directions at the same time. Some lizards have tongues that are longer than their entire bodies, tails that break off in the heat of battle, and skin that can change from brilliant to dull and back again depending on the lizard's sex, the season, or the mood of the individual lizard itself.

Perhaps the most unusual characteristics of all are related to reproduction. Some lizards are capable of reproducing without sex—in other words, they create clones of themselves. Other lizards can actually change the sex of their offspring, depending on the temperature.

If these exploits sound amazing, it is because they *are* amazing! Lizards are remarkable creatures. To find out more about the world of lizards, read on.

2

What Is a Lizard?

To most people, a lizard, at first glance, looks just like a dinosaur. But though the creatures are similar, lizards are not miniature dinosaurs. To appreciate the difference between the two, it is necessary to review the evolution of reptiles, which began millions of years ago.

For about 3 billion years, before reptiles or any other living things appeared on land, life was limited exclusively to the oceans. Plants first appeared on land about 450 million years ago. They were followed quickly by animals. By 400 million years ago, insectlike anthropods had colonized the land. Fifty million years later they were joined by the amphibians, the first land vertebrates.

Moving from the water to the land had its rewards—more food, fewer predators, less competition—but it also had its challenges. The amphibians solved many, but not all, of the problems that animals faced in trying to survive in this new environment.

REPTILES WERE THE FIRST ANIMALS TO MOVE COMPLETELY OUT OF THE WATER. THIS ASIAN WATER DRAGON RETURNS TO THE WATER ONLY IN AN EMERGENCY, DROPPING FROM A BRANCH TO A STREAM OR POOL BELOW TO AVOID A PREDATOR.

For breathing, amphibians evolved lungs that could take oxygen out of the air. For supporting their body weight without the buoyancy of water, amphibians developed a strong arched backbone, or spine, formed of vertebrae. For sensing the outside world, amphibians took on eyes and ears that could function in a non-water environment.

Two tough problems remained. The first was keeping moisture inside the body. Amphibians only partially solved this problem—their skin is not waterproof. When exposed to air for long periods of time, amphibians will lose water and eventually dry out completely. For this reason, amphibians are creatures that must live in wet habitats. If they get too far away from water, they run the risk of losing their lives.

The reptiles were able to solve this "drying out" problem with a series of innovations that made them the first full-time four-footed land animals about 350 million years ago. Rather than trying to survive on land with a thin, porous amphibianlike skin, reptiles developed a body covering made of tough, almost waterproof scales. The scales that reptiles developed gave them much more freedom to colonize the land. While amphibians needed to stay close to the swampy shorelines, reptiles were free to pursue food sources (and find escape routes from enemies) on any land habitat. This gave them a distinct advantage over their amphibian relatives.

The other problem that amphibians did not completely solve involved methods of reproduction. Amphibian reproduction is basically haphazard. The female lays eggs in some underwater habitat—a puddle, a lake, pond, ocean, or stream. These eggs are left unprotected. Many of them are eaten by predators long before a male amphibian can get around to fertilizing them with his sperm, so amphibians need to lay thousands of eggs in the hope that a few will survive.

Once eggs develop, the underwater environment of the juvenile amphibians is still filled with peril. The problems include lots of predators ready to snap them up as soon as they hatch. By the time the juvenile amphibians are old enough to leave the water, only a tiny fraction of the original eggs laid by the female still survive. So for amphibians, reproduction is always very "iffy." Thousands are produced so a few will survive.

These problems were largely "solved" by reptiles with a series of four reproductive innovations. The first major reptile innovation was the process of internal fertilization. While amphibians joined egg and sperm outside of the body in a very unreliable, hit-or-miss process, reptile fertilization was much more of a sure thing. Rather than dump a load of sperm onto a pile of eggs in a constantly changing underwater environment, male reptiles placed their sperm directly inside the female's body, where they were much more likely to reach eggs and fertilize them successfully.

Reptiles' second great reproductive innovation was in keeping the eggs from drying out. Eggs of all types must stay moist to survive. Amphibians solved this problem by laying their eggs in water. Reptiles used a different strategy—rather than bringing the egg to water, reptiles brought water to the egg in the form of a water-filled, protective sac called the amnion. This amniotic egg is an innovation that was adopted by many animals that arose after reptiles, including mammals and birds.

The third major reptile innovation for reproduction was to protect the egg with a tough outer shell. For this reason, reptiles had to make sure that the shell was added to the egg only *after* fertilization took place inside the female's body. Putting a shell around an unfertilized egg would have created a new problem: How could a male deliver sperm to an egg that was locked up in an air-tight package?

LIVING ON THE LAND FULL-TIME BROUGHT NEW OPPORTUNITIES AND DANGERS FOR REPTILES.

The fourth reptile invention for reproduction was the egg yolk. Immature, still-developing amphibians, such as tadpoles, are capable of getting their own food in their underwater environment. On land, reptiles did not have this option, so their eggs were equipped with a nutritious, energy-rich yolk that would serve to feed the embryo before it hatched. This yolk is another advance that was adopted by other vertebrate groups, including birds.

The Age of Reptiles

With all these adaptive innovations in place, reptiles were ready to conquer the land, and conquer they did. The first great spread of reptile species on land took place at the beginning of the Permian era, about 290 million years ago. By the late Triassic period, some 60 to 70 million years later, reptiles had undergone a second great explosion of growth, ushering in the age of dinosaurs. Lizards themselves first began to appear at this time.

How closely related are lizards to dinosaurs? The diagram below shows how the first amniotic animal—a "pre-reptile"—branched into three lines, based on skull formation. The first line, the synapsids (animals with one hole in their skulls), developed into now extinct mammal-like reptiles, which later led to mammals. The second line, the diapsids (two-holed skulls), split into two branches and led to dinosaurs, birds, and modern reptiles. The third line, the anapsids, which had no skull holes, led to several extinct groups, and perhaps turtles.

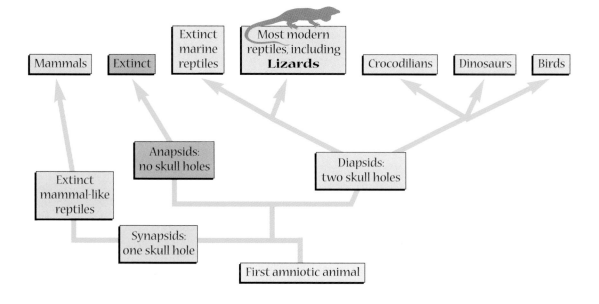

ANIMALS THAT LAID PROTECTED AMNIOTIC EGGS DIVIDED INTO THREE GROUPS, BASED ON THE NUMBER OF SKULL HOLES THEY HAD. LIZARDS, DINOSAURS, BIRDS, AND CROCODILIANS BELONG TO THE DIAPSID GROUP, WHICH HAS TWO SKULL HOLES.

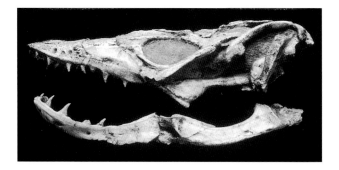

From the diagram on page 23, it is clear that dinosaurs and lizards are related but live on different branches of their family tree. The division exists because of a number of key differences between dinosaurs and lizards. Perhaps the most significant distinction between them involves leg placement. Body structure is a lot like the structure of a building. The stronger the frame, the stronger and more stable the structure itself will be. Lizards have a posture that can be described as a full sprawl—the legs do not lie directly under the body. Therefore lizards are unable to support much body weight.

Contrast the lizard's full sprawl with the semisprawl of a crocodilian. The crocodilian's legs are tucked some of the way under the body, providing stability and support for the animal.

Finally, take a look at the fully improved stance of the dinosaur. The legs are situated directly under the body. The result is that the dinosaur is like a well-supported building. Its upright posture can support a lot more weight than the "unimproved" lizard stance. With better support, dinosaurs were able to grow much larger than lizards and still move with speed and efficiency.

Upright leg placement begins to explain why dinosaurs were able to grow so large and lizards remained small. With a

Full sprawl: lizard   Semisprawl: crocodilian   No sprawl: dinosaur

sprawling posture, there is only so much weight an animal can support. Imagine a lizard that weighed as much as a medium-sized 6,000 pound (2,700 kg) stegosaur. Its bowed-out legs would collapse under its own weight. The largest dinosaurs weighed up to 100 tons (90,000 kg). Imagine trying to support that kind of weight on "lizard legs"!

What remains to be explained is that if the dinosaur body plan was in some way more efficient than that of lizards, why did dinosaurs die out some 65 million years ago—ending the age of reptiles—while lizards were able to survive.

The answer? We don't know. None of the many theories can be proved or disproved. The most favored current theory is that a large asteroid hit Earth at the end of the Cretaceous period. The impact of this object kicked up so much dust that Earth was shrouded in darkness and cold for an extended period of time, killing off not only all dinosaur species but also whole families of plants and animals that then lived on Earth.

Why did lizards survive the cataclysm? Again, scientists can only speculate, but when faced with drastic environmental change, animals often find it is better to be small than large. Large creatures need more food than small ones, and it takes them much longer to reproduce. Whatever the case, the facts remain: the extinction of the dinosaurs left only lizards, turtles, crocodilians, and a few other groups as the only reptiles on Earth.

Modern Lizards

Although the first true lizard, *Prolacerta*, appeared more than 200 million years ago, it was not all that different from lizards that are alive today. Lizards are members of the class Reptilia, which means that they are "cold-blooded" (ectothermic) four-legged vertebrates (though many lizards have two legs or no legs at all) that have dry, scaly skin and give birth to young that look like tiny adult lizards.

Lizards differ from their reptile cousins in a number of ways. As the diagram on page 23 indicates, though modern crocodilians are considered reptiles, they are actually more closely related to birds than they are to lizards. Lizards and crocodilians do bear a strong superficial resemblance to each other, but there are key differences between them. Among those differences are that: (a) lizards shed their skins completely; (b) crocodilians have gizzards; (c) lizards have paired male sex organs; and (d) lizards, as mentioned above, have a more "sprawled" stance than crocodilians.

Lizards are more closely related to snakes than to any of their other reptile relatives. The diagram shown below is a detail of the two diapsid branches of the diagram on page 23.

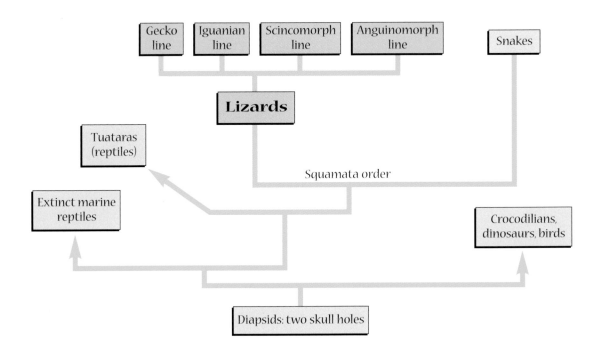

The diagram on page 26 shows that lizards are members of the Squamata order, which includes snakes and lizards. At first glance, distinguishing a lizard from a snake would seem easy and obvious. But in fact there are hundreds of lizards that have reduced legs, or no legs at all. Many of these creatures, such as the glass lizard (*Ophisaurus apodus*), look to the untrained eye almost exactly like a snake. Indeed *O. apodus* is often called the glass snake.

So how do biologists distinguish a lizard from a snake? Lizards have moveable eyelids; snakes don't. Lizards have paired ear openings; again, snakes don't. So if an animal has moveable eyelids and earholes, it's a legless lizard. Fixed eyelids and no earholes means it's a snake. Also, although snakes retain a vestigial pelvic limb girdle where legs were once located, the

THE GROUND MONITOR'S STANCE CLEARLY SHOWS THE LIZARD'S SPRAWLING POSTURE.

girdle appears only at the rear end of the animal. Legless lizards have limb girdles for both front and rear legs.

Ancestral Lines

Understanding lizards as a group is largely a matter of getting to know the various lizard lines. Each line has its own distinct characteristics, but with practice, it is possible to identify different lizard groups and species.

The four groups shown in the diagram on page 26 represent the four basic lizard ancestral lines. These lines can be further subdivided into families that are sometimes quite different in appearance.

The Geckos

Geckos are easy to recognize. Just look for the too-big eyes and the not-so-sleek body shape. With more than 800 different species, this sticky-footed, wall-climbing, insect-devouring lizard group is one of the most successful groups. It is also the group that is probably most closely associated with humans. Geckos, for the most part, show little fear of people. Species such as the Mediterranean gecko, *Hemidactylus turcicus*, or the tokay gecko, *Gekko gecko*, are well-known houseguests in tropical locales, munching on insect pests to the delight of the people who live in those houses. The tokay, often taken in as a house pet, is one of many gecko species that "speaks," making vocal calls that sound like *"Tokay! Tokay!"* to listeners in the night.

Most geckos are nocturnal creatures, staying active during the dark hours and hiding in the day. The exceptions are the more brightly colored day geckos, such as the neon day gecko, *Phelsama klemmeri*. The gecko ancestral line is the most primitive

THE GECKO ANCESTRAL
LINE CONSISTS OF SNAKE
LIZARDS AND MORE THAN
800 GECKO SPECIES,
INCLUDING THIS
MEDITERRANEAN GECKO.

GECKOS THAT COME OUT IN THE DAYTIME, SUCH AS THIS YELLOW-THROATED DAY GECKO
FROM MADAGASCAR, ARE USUALLY BRIGHTER IN COLOR THAN NOCTURNAL GECKOS.

of all lizard and (in some schemes) includes the snake lizards, the pygopodids, which are related to geckos but very different in outward appearance.

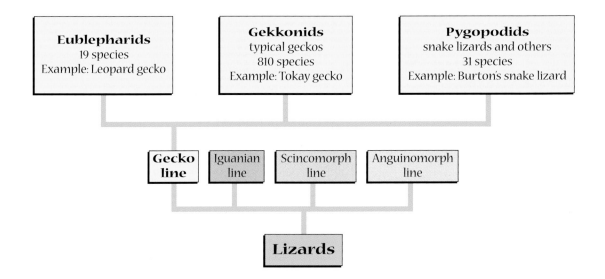

Iguanians. The iguanian line includes more than 1,000 lizard species and three major lizard families: the iguanids, the agamids, and the chameleons. People often get confused between the terms *iguanian, iguanid,* and *iguana. Iguanian* is the name for the entire ancestral line that includes the *iguanids,* the most numerous iguanian subgroup. *Iguana* is the common name for several well-known iguanid species, including the green iguana.

The two main iguanian groups are the iguanids and agamids. Both are extremely similar, but iguanids live only in the Western Hemisphere, while agamids reside in Asia, Europe, Africa, and Australia.

Iguanids and agamids come in all shapes, sizes, and colors. Typically, these lizards are show-offs. They (males especially) often have colorful crests, frills, ruffs, and dewlaps adorning their heads. They also have short tongues and strong, well-developed hind legs.

Iguanid types include the green anole, *Anolis carolinensis*—which is also known as the American chameleon because it can change color—the green iguana, which can grow to huge sizes, and the crevice spiny swift, *Sceloporus poinsettii*. Agamids include the Egyptian thorny-tailed agama, *Uromastyx aegyptius*, and the green water dragon, *Physignathus cocincinus*.

THE IGUANIAN LIZARDS INCLUDE THE IGUANIDS, AGAMIDS, AND THE CHAMELEONS. THIS ANOLE IS A MEMBER OF THE IGUANID FAMILY.

AGAMIDS ARE FOUND ONLY IN ASIA, EUROPE, AFRICA, AND AUSTRALIA.

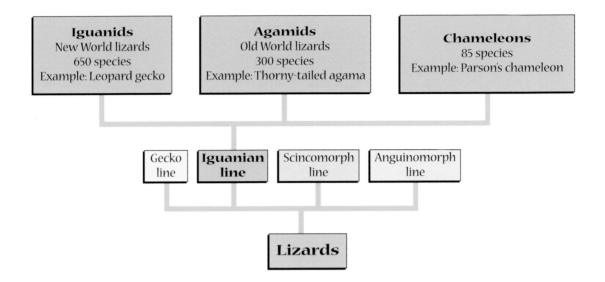

The third branch of the Iguanian line is the chameleon. Chameleons are perhaps the most famous lizards of all, with their ungainly bodies, spectacular color schemes, and sleepy, turretlike eyes, which, among other things, are capable of focusing on two different things at once. One well-known example is Parson's chameleon, *Calumma parsonii*.

Scincomorphs

The scincomorph, or skink, ancestral line, is the largest lizard grouping of all, containing perhaps close to 1,500 different lizard species and six different lizard families. This ancestral line includes three major lizard families, the lacertids, teiids, and skinks, as well as three less common ones.

The relationship between lacertids and teiids is similar to that of the iguanids and agamids: lacertids are Old World (Asian, European, and African) lizards; teiids live only in the New World

THE SCINCOMORPH ANCESTRAL LINE INCLUDES TEIIDS, LACERTIDS, AND SKINKS, AS WELL AS THREE LESS COMMON GROUPS. THIS BLUE-TONGUED SKINK IS A POPULAR PET LIZARD.

(North and South America). Lacertids are sometimes called "typical" lizards. They have long, cylindrical bodies, powerful hind legs, and easily discarded tails. Lacertids are distinguished by a section of large, flat scales on the undersides of their necks. Well-known lacertids include the wall lizard, *Podarcis muralis*, and the common lizard, *Lacerta vivipara*.

Teiids are the New World counterparts to lacertids. Teiids have the same general features and characteristics as lacertids. Typical teiids include the desert grassland whiptail or race runner, *Cnemidophorus uniparens*, and the jungle runner, *Ameiva ameiva*.

Skinks, with their elongated body forms, shiny scales, and quick movements, are some of the easiest lizards to identify. Skinks differ from their lacertid and teiid relatives in two chief ways. In skinks, hind legs tend to be much smaller and less muscular than in the two other groups. An exceptionally long, almost snakelike body form and small, overlapping glossy scales also distinguish the skinks. Typical skinks include the blue-tongued skink, *Tiliqua scincoides*, and the fire skink, *Lygosoma fernandi*.

Other groups within the scincomorph line include the cordylids, the armored girdle-plated lizards, and two less common groups, the night lizards and blind lizards. Cordylids include the sungazer, *Cordylus giganteus*.

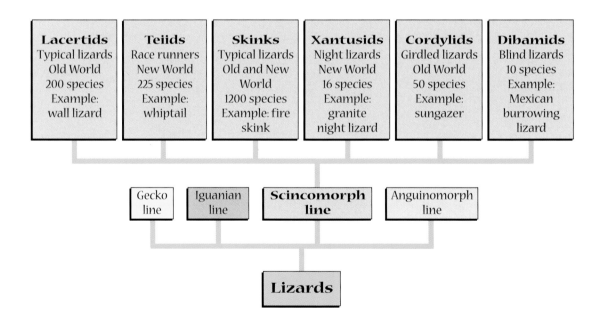

Anguinomorphs. This ancestral line includes the anguids—legless lizards—alligator lizards, and the varanids, or monitor lizards, which include the Komodo dragon and other species with forked tongues.

The best-known anguid is the snakelike glass lizard. Several varanids are well known, including the eight-foot-long perentie, *Varanus giganteus*. Most monitors live in or near Australia. The poisonous beaded lizards, such as the Gila monster, *Heloderma suspectum*, of North America are also anguinomorphs.

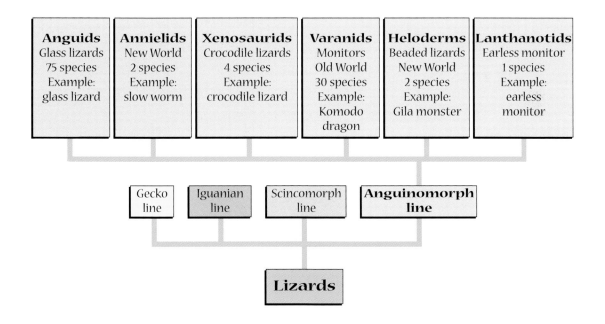

3 The Lizard Body

Lizard bodies come in a wide variety of shapes and sizes to fit almost every lifestyle and habitat. The basic body plan is a marvel of efficient design, and it can be modified by becoming thicker or thinner, longer or shorter, by subtracting or adding legs and such features as frills, crests, thorns, plates, and armor.

Body Structure: A Guided Tour

The most basic lizard body plan is that of a legless glass lizard. To the untrained eye, this creature (an anguid) looks like a snake. But the difference is that glass lizards have earholes and moveable eyelids, two features that distinguish them as lizards.

The sand fish, or Colorado desert fringe-toed lizard (*Uma notata*), a type of skink, has a slightly more complex body form than a snake lizard. The sand fish, essentially a slightly fattened snake with paddles, uses its tiny "paws" to "swim" through sand

THE LEGLESS GLASS LIZARD, A MEMBER OF THE ANGUID FAMILY, IS OFTEN MISTAKEN FOR A SNAKE. ITS MOVEABLE EYE-LIDS AND EAR OPENINGS MARK THIS CREATURE AS A LIZARD.

dunes. Increase the size of the legs, and thicken the torso even more, and you end up with the body contour of the golden skink (*Mabuya multifasciata*). This creature scoots along on the more solid but still sandy soils of its desert home.

Still more developed is the thicker, but still highly streamlined profile of the desert-dwelling rainbow whiptail (*Cnemidophorus lemniscatus*), a teiid lizard from Central America. Compare the whiptail's powerful hind legs to those of the golden skink. The Milos wall lizard (*Podarcis milensis*), a lacertid that lives in dry habitats of southern Europe, is a little bit thicker than the whiptail.

Iguanid and agamid lizards typically adorn their bodies with

TEIIDS AND LACERTIDS ARE VERY SIMILAR, BUT LACERTIDS ARE OLD WORLD LIZARDS, WHILE TEIIDS, SUCH AS THIS ARRUBA ISLAND WHIPTAIL, ONLY LIVE IN NORTH AND SOUTH AMERICA.

head ornaments. While the green anole, an iguanid, has a plain, medium-thick profile, its showy cousin, the brown anole (*Anolis sagrei*) also has a colorful throat fan. The green water dragon, an agamid, has a small crest on top of its head, while the green iguana, an iguanid, has ornaments on both top and bottom. Note the thicker, more muscular body contour of each of these animals, better suited for climbing and moving among vegetation than the elongated bodies of the desert-dwelling skinks and whiptails.

The most spectacular crests of all belong to an iguanid, the brown basilisk (*Basiliscus vittatus)*, and two agamids, the bearded dragon (*Pogona vitticeps)*, and the frilled lizard (*Chlamydosaurus kingii)*. The frilled lizard uses its colossal ruff to shock and intimidate enemies. The brown basilisk, sometimes called the Jesus lizard, is able to run on the surface of water on its two hind legs. The frilled lizard is also capable of moving upright on two legs.

Agamids and iguanids not only have flashy head gear, some species also sport tail ornamentation. Examples include the armadillo lizard (*Cordylus cataphractus)*, a cordylid, and the Egyptian thorny-tailed agama, an agamid. Both of these animals live underground and use their armored tails to plug up the entrance to their burrows as they escape.

Beyond head gear or tail ornaments, some lizards have developed special body modifications that help them glide through the air. The flying lizards, such as the agamid *Draco volans,* the flying dragon, has wings that allow it to take off from high places and soar through the air.

Some lizards have neither sleek nor muscular profiles. The slightly awkward, delicate body shape of the tokay gecko or leopard gecko (*Eublepharis macularius)* seems to suggest gentleness and caution, though geckos are known to be voracious insect eaters. Tokay geckos are commonly seen around human habitations, while leopard geckos are desert dwellers.

THE GECKO BODY PLAN IS LESS STREAMLINED THAN MOST OTHER LIZARD GROUPS. GECKOS CAN ESCAPE ENEMIES BY CLIMBING TO (AND HANGING FROM) PLACES MOST OF THOSE WHO HUNT THEM CANNOT REACH.

The Texas horned lizard, or horned toad *(Phrynosoma cornutum),* and the Australian thorny devil *(Moloch horridus),* have squat shapes. Neither of these creatures would win a beauty contest, but compared with the odd, asymmetrical shapes of chameleons they seem almost ordinary.

Chameleons have undoubtedly the oddest body shape of all lizards. With their skinny legs, chubby bodies, bizarre horns, and droopy turret eyes, chameleons look more like sleepy old wizards than skilled hunters. But make no mistake—chameleons sport tongues that are longer than their bodies, prehensile grasping tails, and odd, "backward" mounted toes that allow them to maneuver through their tree-branch habitats with the greatest of ease.

CHAMELEONS ARE GREAT COLOR CHANGERS, BUT THE COLORS OF THIS PANTHER CHAM-
ELEON HAVE MORE TO DO WITH REPRODUCTION THAN MOOD. MALE CHAMELEONS
SPORT BRIGHT COLORS TO SIGNAL THEIR AVAILABILITY TO FEMALES.

Lizards, Inside and Out

An oddity of lizards is that their behavior can change based on the temperature. Warm lizards can dart around at blazing speeds, while cold lizards sit drowsily in one place, unable to do more than stagger a few steps on weak, shaky legs. Lizards are cold-blooded animals, or ectotherms. If their body temperature falls below its normal optimum—usually between 89.6 and 98.6 degrees Fahrenheit (32° and 37° C)—lizards get sluggish. They become slow not because they do not want to move any faster under these conditions—they can't move any faster.

A lizard must rely on external sources for body heat. Typically, this means it must bask in the sun for a while to warm up. As a rule, a lizard spends the night in its sluggish state, hiding out from predators. When the sun rises and the heat of the day begins, the lizard heats up and becomes highly active, chasing food, avoiding predators, and so on, until darkness falls. Then, since its body temperature may drop to 59 degrees Fahrenheit (15° C) or lower, the lizard once again must hide, falling into an inert, trancelike state.

With a body temperature that can fluctuate by as much as 40 degrees Fahrenheit (22° C) over the course of a single day, how can such an animal survive? How can it possibly compete with its warm-blooded (endothermic) rivals, who maintain the same body temperature (within a few degrees) twenty-four hours a day?

In fact, endotherms do have it better in some ways. In the dark, a lizard in a "slowed-down" state has little ability to defend itself against the likes of a nocturnal predator, such as an owl. An endotherm, such as a mouse, on the other hand, is equally adept at escaping from predators whether it is day or night.

But life is not so easy for endotherms. They pay a large price for maintaining a high body temperature. To keep their body temperature up, they must burn a lot of fuel in the form of food. It is estimated that a small lizard can live a month on the amount of food that an endotherm of equal weight would need to eat in a single *day*. Think about that!

In the end, rather than one form of metabolism being "better" than the other, ectothermy and endothermy are generally thought to be two different strategies that animals use—*both* are efficient, and each has advantages and disadvantages. One surprising fact is that most ectotherms keep their body temperatures at remarkably constant temperatures during their waking hours. Lizards, for example, are masters of changing their location or body angle to get just the right amount of sunshine to stay at their optimum temperature.

Scales and Skin

One trick that lizards use to control their temperature is color change. Dark color absorbs heat better than light color. So when they need to warm up in a hurry, some lizards are capable of changing their skin to a darker color so that it absorbs more energy from the sun.

Color change artists in the lizard world include many anoles (or American chameleons), Indochinese bloodsuckers, and of course, chameleons. Short-term color change is brought about by the secretion of hormones. For chameleons, color change is not generally done for camouflage, as is often mistakenly thought, but rather to reflect the animal's general mood or condition. For example, when a chameleon is challenged by a rival, hormones are secreted into its blood. When these chemicals reach special cells, called chromataphores, in the deep inner skin layers, the cells release pigments that alter the animal's skin color.

Lizard Scales

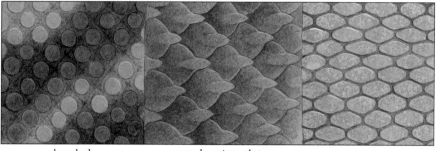

beaded   overlapping plates   scales

Color change may occur for territorial display, to help fight off rivals, to impress female mates, and, least importantly, to match the animal's surrounding environment. All color change eventually shows up on the lizard's outermost skin, or scales. Scale type in lizards varies not only over the range of the 3,000 or so lizard species in the world, but also within a single animal. A lizard such as the eyed lizard (*Lacerta lepida*), has several distinct scale types. On its tail the eyed lizard has keeled scales, which come to a sharp ridge. Its belly features large rectangular scales, while its back is covered with smaller, denser teardrop-shaped units. The top of the eyed lizard's head has irregularly shaped scales, while under its neck it has a collar of large scales, which are typical of all lacertid lizards.

One interesting difference between lizard skin and that of many other animals is that lizard skin doesn't grow. As the animal increases in size, the skin stretches until it reaches the point where it is clearly too small. At this time, the lizard grows listless and sick-looking until, a few days later, it sheds its outer skin and replaces it with a new larger-sized covering, which has grown underneath. The new skin, once it hardens and dries, is brighter and looser than the old, giving the lizard room to grow. Interestingly,

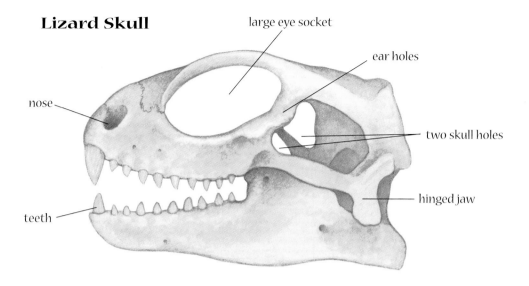

Lizard Skull

large eye socket

ear holes

nose

two skull holes

teeth

hinged jaw

many lizards, such as the green iguana, can keep growing and shedding their skins their entire lives. If these individuals can avoid predators and disease, they can reach immense sizes that rival those of the monitors, the largest lizards on Earth.

Sensory Systems: Eyes, Ears, Nose, and More

Because vision is their primary sense, most lizards have well-developed eyes. The dibamid blind lizards, like many other burrowing species, have eyes that are greatly reduced or covered up by a translucent scale. Many geckos and snake lizards have a transparent scale covering their eyes, making them more similar to snakes than they are to other lizards.

The nocturnal geckos feature exceptionally well-developed and large eyes, consistent with their ability to see in the dark. Geckos can control how much light enters their retina by having one pupil that closes into four different eye holes that they can open and close as needed.

Chameleon eyes have the unique ability to focus on two things at once. When a chameleon is lining up its insect prey prior to an attack, it may keep one turret-shaped eye focused on the prey, while the other eye scans for possible enemies. The instant before the lizard shoots out its extralong tongue at the victim, the second eye will momentarily join the eye that is focused on the prey and zero in for the attack.

In addition to their two normal eyes, many lizards have a "third eye" that is associated with the pineal gland. This eyelike structure is not used for vision. Rather, it monitors daylight conditions and secretes the hormone melatonin to regulate night-day metabolic cycles in the lizard's overall physiology. Melatonin is a hormone that controls such things as sleeping and wakefulness in a variety of species, including human beings.

Not only do lizards have three eyes, some species also have a second "nose"—the Jacobsen's organ at the roof of the mouth. This sensory system, found only in snakes and a few other animal species, functions much like the olfactory (smell) system in other vertebrates. An animal with a Jacobsen's organ uses its

THE EYE OF A CHAMELEON IS BUILT LIKE A SINGLE-REFLEX CAMERA. THE TURRET-SHAPED EYE MOVES UP OR DOWN USING MUSCULAR CONTROL TO CHANGE THE SHAPE OF THE LENS FOR PRECISE FOCUS.

tongue to constantly "taste" the air. The tongue collects molecules from the environment and presses them against sensory cells at the roof of the mouth. From there, messages travel to the animal's brain, telling it, for example, that a predator or prey animal is near.

Legs and Tail

A discussion of the lizard's body would not be complete without a mention of the lizard's most important appendages—its legs and tail.

Though critically important to most lizard species for getting around, legs are optional in some lizard groups. Legless or almost legless lizard species are common in several lizard families. The pygopodid (snake lizards), dibamids (blind lizards), and annelids (burrowing worm lizards) are completely legless. The

Lizard Organs Female Ventral View

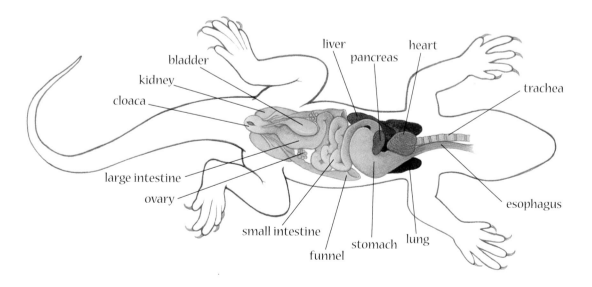

anguids include many species that are legless or have greatly reduced legs, as do the scincids.

In most lizard species, the loss of legs is probably the result of convergent evolution or evolution in which different species have gradually developed similar forms. In this case, different lizards in different habitats, although they did not stem from a common ancestor, gradually developed different lifestyles—usually burrowing—that did not require legs. For example, although Burton's snake lizard, *Lialis burtonis*, and the glass snake, *Ophisaurus apodus*, are not closely related, they both have the same burrowing lifestyle and legless appearance.

Whether legless or not, most lizards get around by wriggling. Lizards with legs run with each diagonally opposite leg moving forward at the same time. Thus, the left front leg and right rear leg move forward together as a pair, as do the right front and left rear legs. In action, this pattern creates a wriggling

Lizard Skeleton

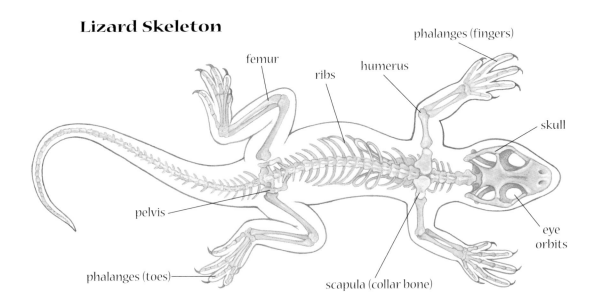

motion, which is not that different from the wriggling motion that legless lizards use to transport themselves through soil or sand.

Tails are a critical appendage for all lizards. Though some species, such as the knob-tailed gecko, *Nephrurus levis*, have short, bulbous tails, many other lizards have tails that are as long as or longer than their bodies. Typically, the lacertid (Old World) and teiid (New World) lizards, such as wall lizards, race runners, and whiptails, have extremely long tails.

Lizards typically use their tails as a counterbalance for climbing and running. Species that do a lot of climbing through tree branches and other forms of vegetation stick out their tails much the way a tightrope walker uses a pole—to redistribute their weight in the opposite direction than that in which they might be likely to fall. Many lizard species, such as the Solomon Islands skink, *Corucia zebrata, Naultinus* geckos, and most chameleons, have prehensile tails—tails used for grabbing—in most cases to right themselves or to avoid falling from high places.

4 Lizards in Action

Lizards move around a lot. They are often seen darting from one location to the next, moving so fast that the eye can barely follow. Compared with other reptile groups, such as the crocodilians, which lie motionlessly for extended periods of time, or even snakes, lizards are positively bursting with energy. What are lizards so busy doing? In what seems like constant motion, lizards are usually involved in one of two activities—looking for prey, or avoiding predators.

Food Sources

Most lizards are carnivores, although their tastes run heavily toward insects or invertebrates rather than more "meaty" vertebrate food sources. Some lizards will eat many small animals, including insects, spiders, mites, snails, scorpions, worms, as well as fruits and vegetables and the eggs of other animals. These omnivorous lizards contrast with species that are very

THOUGH OFTEN SLOW AND AWKWARD, CHAMELEONS CATCH AN AMAZING AMOUNT OF PREY, PRIMARILY BECAUSE OF THEIR KEEN EYE-SIGHT AND LONG-RANGE TONGUE. THE END OF THE TONGUE HAS A STICKY MUCUS TIP TO MAKE SURE THAT PREY CANNOT GET AWAY.

specific in what they hunt, preferring to take only one kind of prey in one specific location of their habitat, sometimes during only one time of the day. Still other lizards eat only vegetables, though their numbers are small compared with the hunters of the lizard world.

Insects are by far the most common prey in almost every lizard family. Geckos are famous for eating insects, especially flies and cockroaches. Families that feature insect eaters, or are largely made up of insect eaters, include the pygopodids (snake lizards), iguanids, agamids, chameleons, lacertids, teiids, varanids (monitors), cordylids (armored lizards), heloderms (poisonous lizards), and skinks.

THE TOKAY GECKO IS AN AMBUSHER. IT WAITS IN A SINGLE PLACE WHERE PREY ARE LIKELY TO COME. WAITING NEXT TO AN INSECT-ATTRACTING LIGHT BULB, THIS LIZARD IS UNLIKELY TO GO HUNGRY FOR LONG.

Among the geckos and closely related pygopodids, most species are insect or spider eaters. An exception is the Burton's snake lizard, which is notorious for eating skinks. Another pygopodid, *Pygopus nigriceps*, focuses on scorpions. The tokay gecko eats small rodents as well as insects.

UNLIKE MOST LIZARDS, CHUCKWALLAS ARE PRIMARILY HERBIVORES. THEY SEEM TO HAVE A DISTINCT FONDNESS FOR YELLOW FLOWERS, BUT EAT PLANTS OF MANY VARIETIES.

Most iguanids, such as anoles and swifts, are insect eaters, but some of the largest iguanid species, such as the green iguana and the chuckwalla, feed only on plant material. Among the agamids, the spiny tail lizards and the bearded dragons are plant eaters.

Lizards that eat other lizards include the eastern collared lizard, a type of swift, the eyed lizard, a lacertid, a few of the larger skinks, many different chameleon species, and many monitor lizards.

The typical agamid is a wide-ranging insect eater, but some agamids, such as the thorny devil, are very particular about what they consume. This animal will eat only ants of a particular genus, and when it finds them it may eat up to 3,000 at a single sitting.

Skinks feed on a large variety of prey. The stump-tail, *Trachydosaurus rugosus*, for example, may dine on snails, fruits, leaves, and dead animals, as well as insects. But monitors eat an even more diverse array. Though they are primarily scavengers, larger monitors have been known to kill and eat such varied prey as wild boars, small deer, and rodents.

Hunting Strategies

As hunters, lizards are generally one of two types: searchers or ambushers. Searchers are animals that actively forage through their environment, seeking out prey or other food sources wherever they go. Ambushers are less active animals that go to a single location and wait for the prey to come to them.

Some gecko species, iguanid swifts (also called spiny lizards), teiid race runners and whiptails, lacertid wall lizards, and eyed lizards are searchers.

The eyed lizard is an example of an extremely active

THE ZEBRA-TAILED LIZARD, NORTH AMERICA'S FASTEST SPECIES, OFTEN WAVES ITS
TAIL CONSPICUOUSLY AT PREDATORS. THIS SIGNALS TO THE PREDATOR THAT THE
LIZARD IS AWARE THAT IT PLANS TO ATTACK. SINCE IT CANNOT SURPRISE THE LIZARD,
IT MAY AS WELL GIVE UP.

species, hunting down a wide variety of prey, including insects,
small birds and rodents, and smaller lizards. This creature is also
known to feed on eggs, fruits, and vegetables. In a similar way,
the teiid rainbow whiptail is a furiously active hunter, searching
constantly for insects, grubs, worms, and spiders.

In contrast, the zebra-tailed lizard (*Callisaurus draconoides*), a southwestern desert iguanid, prefers to sit and wait until suitable prey—a bug or grasshopper—happens by. Then it springs into action on its long legs, sprinting at a top speed of 18 miles per hour (30 kmh) to catch its prey, gobbling it down, then returning to the safety of its perch.

Many house gecko species also sit and wait for their prey. These animals are often found in and around habitats that are lived in by humans. Their hunting strategy is to sit on a vertical surface—usually a wall—near an electric light and wait for the insects to gather. The vertical surface gives the geckos safety from predators. And the light, which insects are naturally attracted to, provides an abundance of prey that geckos will pick off one by one, feasting on until the night comes to an end.

Some of the most specialized feeders include the horned toad and other *Phrynosoma* lizards from North American desert habitats. These slow-moving predators typically sit at the edge of an ant trail and wait for the ants to come by, gobbling up as many as 3,000 of the insects at a single sitting. Horned toads eat so many ants that their stomachs are much larger than those of other lizards, just to accommodate the quality of largely indigestible material that they must process each day. Recent research has shown that horned toads are such particular eaters that they refuse to dine on a foreign ant species that has displaced some native ants in California. Scientists are worried that the new ants may cause horned toads to become a threatened species.

Defense Strategies

When lizards aren't hunting food, they are usually trying to avoid predators. Lizards are an important link in many food chains, serving as prey for a variety of attackers, including birds,

THE THORNY DEVIL'S UNAPPETIZING APPEARANCE DRIVES AWAY MOST PREDATORS.

such as owls, eagles, and hawks, mammals, such as hedgehogs, pigs, cats, raccoons, and other reptiles, such as snakes and other lizards.

The evolutionary struggle between predator and prey is never ending. If the prey becomes faster or stronger, the predator usually stays in step. One adaptation begets another. Over the long run, this means that predator and prey populations stay in balance. Both sides survive, but neither side gains an overwhelming advantage.

Over time, lizards have developed two basic strategies for avoiding predators.

Defense Strategy 1: Don't Get Noticed.

Lizards are not particularly strong, fast, or clever when compared with predators such as eagles or hawks. Once spotted, lizards often have difficulty getting away from their enemies. So for the vast majority of lizard species, the best defense is to remain invisible.

Camouflage and Illusion. Camouflage, the art of blending in with one's surroundings, is the primary way in which many lizards avoid detection. The Australian leaf-tailed gecko, *Phyllurus cornutus*, provides a superb example of how hard it is to spot a well-camouflaged lizard.

But camouflage need not be perfect to provide protection. For example, in a desert habitat that presents a wide variety of sun-bleached features, it is often better to have a basic match to the surroundings—a light color in a generally light setting, for example—than the perfectly matched camouflage exhibited by the Australian leaf-tailed gecko. That gecko may blend into some parts of the environment but stick out conspicuously in others. In a varied environment, general camouflage suited to all surroundings is better than a perfect camouflage suited to only one environment.

Camouflage isn't just a matter of color. Perhaps more important is how the pattern of color and light-and-dark is arranged—in spots, blotches, streaks, and stripes—to match the surrounding environment. This kind of irregular coloration is used throughout the animal kingdom, as well as by human hunters and military personnel. The best way to blend in with an uneven, broken-up environment is with an uneven and irregular color-pattern camouflage.

Many lizards, such as the whiptail and the six-lined race runner, feature long, horizontal lines that run along the length of the animal's body. These lines serve not so much to camouflage

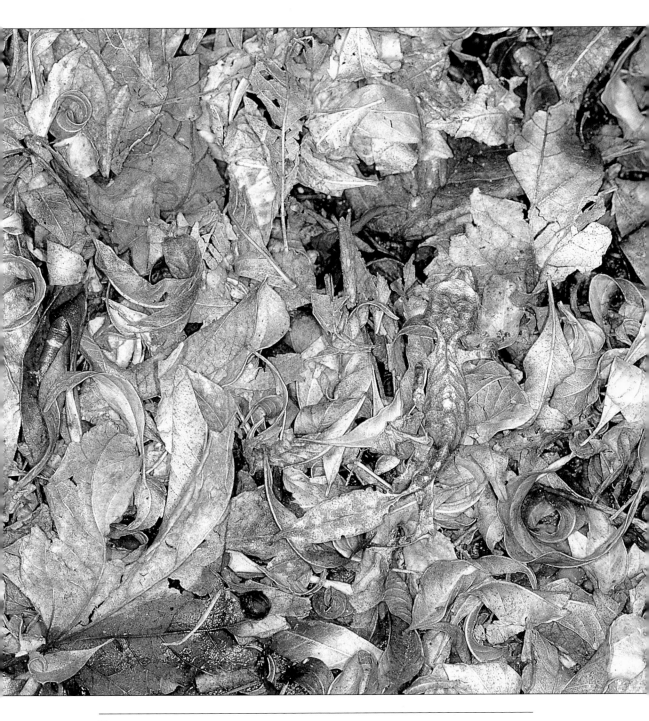

THE CAMOUFLAGE OF THE LEAF-TAILED GECKO IS ALMOST PERFECT.

the animal as to create an optical illusion when the animal is in motion. Moving lines confuse the enemy. When the predator sees a shifting horizontal pattern skittering along the surface, it has difficulty judging just where the front or back of the prey is and how to get the best angle of attack.

Movement and Shadow. The visual systems of most predators are tuned to detect motion more than anything else. Most predators will attack whatever moves, finding out only afterward whether what they have caught is worth eating. To avoid being noticed, lizards and other prey animals learn to move in specialized ways. Rather than run at a steady, fluid pace, lizards move in a darting, herky-jerky way. They sprint, then stop, stay motionless, sprint again, then stop again, all the while trying to minimize the amount of time that they can be seen in motion.

Most lizards also move very close to the ground. Raising their bodies up high can expose them in two ways. First, it exposes their often brightly colored underbody to the predator. Second, and just as importantly, raising themselves up creates dark shadows that can catch a predator's eye.

Concealment. Perhaps the best way to avoid being seen is to stay out of sight. Unfortunately, many lizards do not have this option, as their daily basking and food-hunting chores require them to be outside—and seen. Nevertheless, these animals employ a variety of techniques to hide as best they can.

Lizards will stay on the far side of a rock, stump, bush, or other obstruction, away from any observer. Chameleons, otherwise slow and ponderous, also seem to be experts at shifting to the other side of the tree branch they're on, always staying just out of sight.

Of course, ducking behind objects gets an animal only so far. The best hiders among the lizards are the animals that burrow. Some species, including many of the legless lizards, such as the annelids, spend virtually their entire lives underground in a burrow. Burrow life, of course, has its pluses and minuses. On the positive side, few predators notice an animal that stays underground, so many burrow dwellers can be slow-moving creatures, never needing to worry about escaping from a speedy enemy. On the negative side, a burrow dweller must be able to find food in its underground habitat. It is for this reason that most burrowers are somewhat particular eaters, often focusing exclusively on prey that they find in their hidden habitat.

Defense Strategy 2: If You Do Get Noticed, Take Action.

Once seen, each lizard species has its own particular way of dealing with the situation. Though some of these defense methods are successful, many are not, so lizards often end up as prey. To avoid that fate, lizards use three basic strategies.

Deception. Deception is always a gamble. If it works, the animal gets away. If the enemy is not deceived, the prey is left standing in an exposed position without any means of escape.

Once seen, one way to fool a predator is to look unappetizing. The Australian agamid called the thorny devil is so thorny and spike-covered that when it freezes most predators cannot distinguish it from a cactus. Other lizard species use a similar strategy, crouching along the ground to impersonate twigs, branches, and other inedible objects.

Mimicry is well known among insects such as butterflies, which sometimes impersonate fierce or bad-tasting species to ward off enemies. However, very few lizards use mimicry to deceive. One that does is an African lacertid, *Heliobolus lugubris*, a species that imitates a bad-tasting local beetle. Three pygopodid snake lizards of the genus *Delma* are thought to be mimics of venomous snakes, imitating their coloration and the way that snakes raise their heads before they attack.

A gecko from Pakistan, *Teratolepsis fasciata*, has a tail that is said to resemble the head of a poisonous viper. But more common among lizards is using the tail as "bait" for a predator. Several species of skink, lacertid, and teiid lizards have bold-colored tails that attract attention. When threatened, instead of running, these lizards wiggle their tails teasingly, daring their enemies to attack.

When the predator jumps at the bait, the entire tail snaps off from the lizard's body in a clean break, leaving the lizard to escape and the predator with only a wriggling tail. That's right—many lizards have special tail muscles that are designed to keep wriggling even *after* the tail snaps off, assuring that the lizard gets away.

Defensive tail loss is quite common among lizard species, though some species are more likely to lose their tails than others. Indeed, there are skink populations in which tail loss is so common that it is difficult to find an individual that does *not* sport the signs (discoloration and shape) of a regrown tail. Some snakes, in fact, are said to feed almost entirely not on lizards, but just on their tails. There are also skinks that are known to eat their own tails.

Escape. If deception fails, a lizard in most cases has no choice but to run. Lizards, for the most part, seem faster than they actually are. In general, 20 miles per hour (32 kmh) is about the upper limit for any squamata reptile. In many instances this speed allows lizards to escape even the most wily of predators—that and their elusiveness and unpredictability. However, when a lizard is being chased by a bird or some other faster creature, it often loses the battle.

To increase their chances of escape, some lizard species, such as the iguanid, *Uta stansburiana*, the common side-blotched lizard, do not venture far from their burrows. If spotted, they are never more than a few feet from safety, and they dash to their holes just ahead of the predator.

The agamids of the *Uromastyx* genus have spiked tails. When these lizards are chased to their burrows they leave their armored tails sticking up, deterring even the boldest enemy from trying to pry them out. The even more heavily armored sungazer defends itself in a similar way. The armadillo lizard will grab its own spiky tail in its mouth, forming a hoop-shaped shield to ward off attackers.

Hiding between rocks is a common way for lizards such as the crevice spiny lizard to escape enemies, but the chuckwalla takes this strategy one step further. When threatened, the chuckwalla retreats to a gap between rocks, where it then puffs up its entire body with air, making it so "fat" that it becomes wedged between the rocks and is impossible to remove. (The species name for *S. obesus* accurately describes this creature.)

But some fleeing lizards do not stay on land for safety. The green water dragon perches on branches above a stream or creek. When threatened, it drops into the water and swims away. The brown basilisk has a unique escape route: rather than swim through water, it walks—on two feet—right over water. The sand fish, on the other hand, dives right below the surface to escape—except the surface it breaks is not water, but sand. Nevertheless, using its snakelike body, a sand fish can usually wriggle away to safety.

Bluffing. Lizards, for the most part, are not capable of overpowering their predators. Nevertheless, they sometimes have no choice but to fight back when they are attacked.

The most spectacular display of aggression is carried out by the frilled lizard. When not threatened, this creature keeps its ruff folded up around its throat. But if an enemy approaches, the creature inflates its ruff into an enormous structure that could strike terror into the heart of even the fiercest predator. If the enemy refuses to be intimidated, the frilled lizard has little to back up its ploy, but in most cases the bluff works and the frilled lizard prevails.

Other lizards try less dramatic bluffs, such as making aggressive motions, rising up into the air, or making intimidating noises. The Mediterranean gecko moves its tail from side to side when threatened, creating a disturbing hissing noise. The blue-tongued skink waits until its enemy is about to pounce, then reveals its shockingly blue tongue. This tactic probably surprises the enemy more than anything else, but it is usually enough to give the animal time to escape.

The Gila monster and Mexican beaded lizard are the only two poisonous lizards in the world. Few predators ever get near either of these two creatures—their bright colors provide a loud and clear signal to any prospective predator that they are armed and dangerous.

The most bizarre defense mechanism of all is the horned

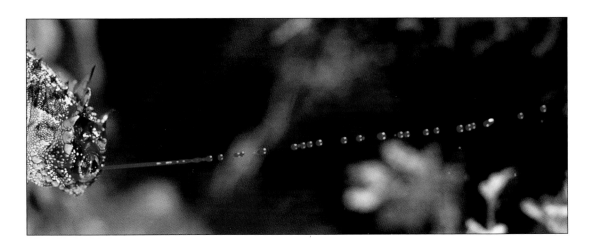

THE ULTIMATE SHOCK DEFENSE: A TEXAS HORNED LIZARD SHOOTS BLOOD AT AN ATTACKER. THIS DEFENSE ACTUALLY BURSTS THE SINUS WALLS AROUND THE LIZARD'S EYES.

lizard's tactic of squirting blood out of its eyeballs at enemies. This ploy is apparently used not to harm the enemy, but to put such an unpleasant taste in its mouth that it no longer wants to have anything to do with its quarry.

5 Getting to Know Lizards

The best way to understand lizards is to get to know some of them in more depth. Here are brief profiles of some well-known lizards that are representative of their groups.

Tokay Gecko, *Gekko gecko* (gecko)

The call of "To-kay! To-kay!" is a familiar sound in the southeast Asian habitats of this well-known gecko. The colorful tokay is one of the largest geckos, measuring as much as 14 inches (35 cm) in length. Its soft skin and sticky feet are typical gecko features, though the tokay's bright colors are quite unusual for a nocturnal gecko, which usually get by in the darkness with a drab outer appearance.

The cries of "To-kay!" and "Ge-ko!" are not just idle noise. As night creatures, geckos do not rely on visual displays for courtship. Instead, like frogs, the males sing to attract mates. Tokays are solitary creatures, keeping to themselves except during mating

"TOKAY! TOKAY!" THOUGH NOT PARTICULARLY GOOD-NATURED, TOKAYS ARE POPULAR AS PETS. WHEN ANGRY, THEY EMIT A SHARP HISSING SOUND.

season. Females are generally smaller and less brightly colored than males. Like all other geckos, they lay one to two eggs. Males are known to fight, and a tokay can inflict painful bites on its enemies—including human handlers!

Tokays are typically found in trees (their natural habitat) or buildings. As geckos, tokays have the ability to stick to vertical wall surfaces, and even hang upside down on a glass surface. Although a microscopic look at gecko feet shows tiny cuplike structures, geckos do not use suction to attach themselves to things. Geckos do not, for instance, stick to a wet, smooth surface such as glass. Instead, the secret to their stickiness appears to be that the tiny structures form an electric attraction to the surfaces on which they adhere.

Bearded Dragon, *Pogona vitticeps* (agamid)

Who wouldn't back down in a face-off against one of these creatures? This fierce 2-foot-long (60-cm) customer hails from Australia, and its appearance is quite imposing. The bearded dragon's bluff is probably worse than its bite, though. The dragon may be feisty, but the main purpose of its spiky beard and open-mouthed gape is to intimidate.

When threatened, the dragon's beard inflates to an impressive size and turns a dark and angry (usually purple) color. Both males and females have beards, and both use them for aggression and courtship behavior. To show their readiness to mate, males will bob their heads slowly to gain acceptance from females. Pregnant females will lay up to twenty-four eggs that take about sixty-five days to hatch.

Bearded dragons make excellent pets, often engaging in curious hand-waving behavior. When doing this, the lizard stands on three legs and rotates its front leg in a circular pattern,

BEARDED DRAGONS WILL EAT ALMOST ANYTHING, INCLUDING PLANTS, INSECTS, AND EVEN SMALL RODENTS. BEARDED DRAGONS ARE POPULAR AS PETS BECAUSE OF THEIR PLEASANT TEMPERAMENT.

much like a person waving hello or good-bye. What is the meaning of this unusual behavior? Scientists think that hand-waving helps members of the species recognize one another. Hand-waving may also be a way that the lizards show dominance over one another.

Horned Toads, *Phrynosoma solare, P. cornutum* (iguanid)

These small, 5-inch (13-cm) lizards strike a squat and almost comical pose, resembling toads more than they do other lizards.

Native to the deserts of Mexico and the southeastern United States, they have a number of remarkable characteristics that mark them as special among lizard species.

Horned toads are ant eaters, for the most part, shooting out their long, sticky tongues and gobbling up hundreds of ants at a time. Horned toads will eat other insects, but harvester ants are their favorite prey, occupying 88 percent of their stomach contents, according to a recent study. Horned toads are hot-weather lizards. They typically begin their day by basking in the sun for an hour or more. When their internal temperature reaches its optimum, they begin to forage for food. Like other

NINETY PERCENT OF THE HORNED TOAD'S DIET CONSISTS OF HARVESTER ANTS, MIXED IN WITH A FEW OTHER INSECTS AND SPIDERS.

lizards, horned toads run the risk of overheating—if they stay in the sun for too long they often need to retreat to shade during the heat of the day. These creatures have the ability to change their skin color, turning lighter or darker, depending on their environment and how much heat energy they need to absorb.

When enemies or possible mates approach, horned toads revert to typical behavior patterns, bobbing their heads, doing slow-motion push-ups, and rocking back and forth. When enemies do not back down, horned toads mount a unique defense. By restricting blood flow in their heads to the eye region, they build up such high pressure that blood will come spurting out at the enemy, up to a distance of 3.5 feet (1 meter).

Green Iguana, *Iguana iguana* (iguanid)

These beauties are perhaps the best-known, most-owned, and most-abused reptiles in the world. With their regal crests, showy dewlaps, and sharp, craggy claws, iguanas have been used as models for numerous dinosaur and monster movies. Though they look scary enough, iguanas are for the most part vegetarians, feeding on fruits, leaves, flowers, and sometimes insects. In captivity, it has been said that iguanas will even snatch the occasional slice of pizza or dish of ice cream.

Hunted for their skin, eggs, and meat, iguanas are one of the few lizards that provide a significant food source for people in South American forests. However, an even greater danger to iguanas than hunting is the pet trade. Each year, close to 2 million iguanas are imported into the United States alone. Iguanas make terrific house pets for those who have the knowledge and space to keep them. But only a fraction survive, as in many cases, owners of iguanas do not know how to care for their pets, and the lizards end up being mistreated, ignored, or dumped.

MALE IGUANAS SPEND QUITE A BIT OF TIME AND ENERGY TRYING TO GAIN DOMINANCE OVER ONE ANOTHER FOR THE RIGHT TO MATE. IN CAPTIVITY, THIS TYPE OF BEHAVIOR OFTEN MAKES IGUANAS HARD TO CONTROL.

Aggressiveness is a major problem that some pet owners experience with their iguanas. In the wild, aggression helps iguanas express their dominance, especially during the mating season. But in a home, an overly aggressive iguana is much like an overly aggressive dog—and iguanas can be larger than many dogs. In the wild, iguanas are one of several lizard species that seem to have no limit on their growth. If an iguana can manage to avoid predators and disease when young, it can occasionally grow to lengths of 6.5 feet (2 meters).

Flying Dragon, *Draco volans* (agamid)

Imagine a lizard that can scale the top of a high tree branch, leap into the air, then swoop to the ground like a bold daredevil.

The flying dragon does not really fly, but it glides through the air effortlessly, like a living kite swooping to the ground. The secret to the dragon's gliding ability is its pair of winglike flaps, which open up in response to air resistance.

How did the flying dragon ever develop wings in the first place? Scientists speculate that the wings first appeared as enlarged frills that turned out to be useful for extending a jump. Interestingly, the flying dragon's aerial ability is used only for locomotion and never for escape. When threatened, the lizard does not jump but climbs ever higher in its tree-branch habitat.

Male and female flying dragons are approximately the same size and grow to about 18 inches (48 cm). The males have a

FLYING DRAGONS SIGNAL THAT THEY ARE ABOUT TO FLY BY POINTING THEIR HEADS TOWARD THE GROUND. THEN THEY TAKE OFF INTO THE AIR. A TYPICAL FLIGHT FOR ONE OF THESE CREATURES MEASURES ABOUT 98 FEET (30 M) IN LENGTH.

bright yellow dewlap, while the female dewlap is smaller and bluish gray. Male dragons are extremely territorial. Dominant males stake out as their territory an area that includes two or three trees—usually those that contain female dragons.

Chuckwalla, *Sauromalus obesus* (iguanid)

This chubby southeastern desert dweller gets its odd name from a Shoshone Indian word that was used by Native Americans in southern California. The chuckwalla is an ungainly creature, usually waddling awkwardly as it forages along the ground. But chuckwallas are capable of moving at surprisingly high speeds and of leaping long distances from rock to rock.

About a foot and a half in length (50 cm), chuckwallas are the second largest lizards in the United States, and like green iguanas, eat a mostly vegetarian diet. Chuckwallas seem to be especially fond of yellow flowers, but they also eat fruits, leaves, and plant stems.

Chuckwallas defend themselves primarily by running between rocks, where they wedge themselves in tightly. When threatened, chuckwallas can inflate their lungs up to three times their normal volume. This fattens the animal so much that enemies find it virtually impossible to pry the lizard loose from between the rocks.

Anoles, *Anolis* genus (iguanids)

In their tropical Caribbean home ranges, anoles come in sizes ranging from 8 inches to 16 inches (20 to 40 cm) and in a variety of different shades of brown, green, gray, tan, and blue. Some are jumpers, others are climbers; some are shy, hiding and avoiding being seen, while others are bold. Almost all of

To wedge itself between rocks, a chuckwalla inflates its lungs to three times their normal capacity. This balloon shape keeps the chuckwalla from being dislodged by enemies.

them are lightning fast, darting this way and that. They live in every possible niche: in trees, on trees, under trees, on fences, in houses and bushes, and in the grass. They also spend a lot of time climbing over rocks.

Florida is the home of the green anole, *Anolis carolinensis,* a species that is often called the "American chameleon" because of its ability to change body color. Recently, new anole species from the West Indies, such as *A. sagrei*, the brown anole, and *A. equestris*, the knight anole, have been introduced in Florida and are taking over the green anole's habitats.

Anoles are widely studied by biologists because they provide valuable information on how evolution operates. Presumably, within a habitat a single anole species can diversify into several "specialist" species: one species in the tree canopy, a second species populating the tree trunk, and even a third species patrolling the bottom part of the tree. Each species will be specialized for its particular niche: the tree dweller might have strong legs for jumping from branch to branch; the bottom dweller might have short legs for hiding and maneuvering through twigs in the underbrush.

Even more interestingly, different anoles appear to occupy the same niche on different islands. So *A. gundlachi*, a long-legged island species, might occupy the same position and niche on a tree trunk that a similar but slightly different long-legged species occupies on a different island. This is an example of convergent evolution, where different species develop similar adaptations to survive in similar habitats.

Jackson's Chameleon, *Chamaeleo jacksonii* (chameleonid)

Looking like a curious creature out of a *Star Wars* movie, this East African lizard is only one of the amazing group of creatures that are called chameleons. Its horns make Jackson's chameleon a standout even among its chameleon cousins—and they're not just for show. When rival males square off for battle to win mating privileges, they charge horns first, attempting to dislodge the enemy from its perch on a tree branch.

THE THREE HORNS OF A MALE JACKSON'S CHAMELEON ARE MUCH LARGER THAN
THOSE OF THE FEMALE. MALES FIGHT ONE ANOTHER WITH THEIR HORNS DURING
BATTLES FOR COURTSHIP RIGHTS.

There is not much about chameleons that is not amazing.
From head to toe, these lizards are loaded with fascinating features. On their feet, chameleons have zygodactylous toes—two
toes point inward, the other three point outward—to give the
animal a better grip on a tree branch. Chameleon tails are prehensile, so the lizard can secure itself on its tree-branch perch.

Even more remarkable are the lizard's eyes. Each eye separately scans the environment for the chameleon's favorite prey—spiders and insects. As one eye draws a bead on the victim, the other surveys a full 180 degrees of the background, keeping a lookout for enemies. When the prey gets within range, the chameleon's amazing sticky-ended tongue shoots out, spearing the target in the blink of an eyelash. The tongue, which is one-and-a-half times the body length of the lizard, hits its mark in one-sixteenth of a second, which is too fast for even the quickest of victims to escape.

Last but not least are the colors of chameleons. When they are provoked, upset, or challenged, chameleons will undergo a color change. For example, when two Jackson's males square off to fight, they will both display—inflating their bodies to maximum size, thrusting their heads forward, and opening their mouths to reveal dazzling colors within. While the winner of the battle stays brilliant, the loser turns dull and drab, cowering and shrinking in defeat.

Mating rituals are similar to fight behaviors. Males will flash their brilliance—usually enhanced and intensified during mating season—to females. If the female boldly flashes back at the male, it means she is not interested. If her behavior is less bold, it signals the male to press on and complete the mating process.

Frilled Lizard, *Chlamydosaurus kingii* (agamid)

Of all the horrible-looking monsters that have ever walked the face of the Earth, this 33-inch (84-cm) native of Australia and New Guinea has to be one of the scariest of them all. Like a superhero with a secret identity, the frilled lizard seems anonymous as it goes about its business of looking for insects and spiders, its cape tucked safely around its shoulders. But get this creature disturbed and it shows the ability to shock even the most unflappable of observers.

Typically, the frilled lizard will run on two legs like a frantic escaped prisoner and then, at the key moment, turn and flash the most frightening open-mouthed roar, all the while making hideous hissing sounds. If this doesn't drive an enemy away, nothing will!

The frilled ruff is the lizard's most spectacular feature, measuring some 12 inches (30 cm) across. Besides using it for defensive purposes, both males (whose ruff is larger) and females display their ruffs during courtship.

Komodo Dragon, *Varanus komodoensis* (varanid)

Want to know what it was like when giants roamed the Earth? Come to the small Indonesian island of Komodo (and two other nearby islands) to see a living giant, the heavyweight champion of the entire lizard world—the Komodo dragon. How big is this creature? If it stood upright, it could use its nose to block basket-ball shots from going into the basket. On all fours, it would have trouble fitting into many bedrooms, though it is hard to imagine anyone who would invite this beast through the door. At 10.3 feet (3.1 m), the Komodo dragon is so big that in addition to preying on small mammals and carrion it also hunts and kills 200-pound (90-kg) deer! Think of it: a *lizard* eating a *deer!*

Discovered by westerners in 1910 and known among the local islanders as the *ora*, to the outside world the dragon usually goes by the name of its home island: Komodo. Unlike some lizards that are simply fierce-looking, the Komodo is just as dangerous as it is large. Observers agree that when the Komodo decides to attack, nothing can stop it.

As if its great size and powerful limbs weren't enough, the Komodo is equipped with another "secret" weapon: Its bite contains deadly strains of bacteria. If its prey gets bitten but manages to escape, in most cases it will soon die of an infection. Interestingly, Komodos themselves do not develop infections when they are attacked, as often happens, by larger Komodos. They seem to have an immunity that keeps the bacteria from growing.

Another notable Komodo trait is the ability to "taste" the air. Sticking out its forked tongue (a key characteristic of the varanids, or monitor lizards) and swaying its head back and forth, the Komodo draws in scent molecules to its highly sensitive Jacobsen's organ on the roof of its mouth, giving it the ability to detect prey or rotting meat up to 5 miles (8 km) in the distance.

Komodos reproduce like other lizards. Males fight for dominance, going back on two legs and wrestling one another for the right to court a female. The female is known to sit on her eggs, but not to care for her young after they are born. Baby Komodos are tiny, weighing in at a mere 3 ounces (85 g).

Gila Monster, *Heloderma suspectum* (helodermatid)

The 2-foot-long (60-cm) Gila monster is the largest lizard in the United States and the only poisonous one. Ranging through the deserts of the Southwest, the Gila monster feeds on hatchling birds, reptiles, and young mammals. It lives almost its entire existence underground, emerging only in the spring months to breed and feed. The lizard's venomous bite, which contains a neurotoxin that poisons the nerve cells of its victim, is probably used only for defensive purposes. The Gila monster has no need to inject poison into prey that is already helpless.

The bright colors of the Gila monster serve to warn enemies

THE GILA MONSTER SPENDS MORE THAN 95 PERCENT OF ITS TIME UNDERGROUND
HUNTING FOR EGGS AND THE YOUNG OF OTHER BURROWING ANIMALS.

that it is poisonous. Though normally slow and lethargic, the
Gila monster can move quickly in emergencies. When
approached, it lets out a frightening hiss.

6 Reproduction

Reptiles were able to emerge from the water and become the first large full-time land animals primarily because they used a new method of reproduction. Unlike amphibians, female reptiles don't lay hundreds or thousands of unfertilized eggs in the open. Instead, reptile fertilization is internal, and many reptiles lay just one or two eggs at a time. These characteristics illustrate the general strategy that higher animals use for reproduction: invest *more* time and energy in *fewer* offspring.

In many ways, lizard reproductive behavior more closely resembles the behavior of birds than that of fish, amphibians, or even other reptiles. Like birds, courtship and mating for lizards is colorful and complex. Visual display of crests, colors, and other ornaments is an important part of the selection process for lizards, as it is with birds. Male lizards also show a birdlike struggle for territory and dominance. What lizards don't seem to share with birds is maternal behavior. Birds spend a great deal of time

Among anole males, a large, bright throat fan is a flashy status symbol that intimidates other males and impresses females.

and energy caring for their offspring, while in lizards this behavior is mostly absent.

What advantages do elaborate reproductive rituals provide for lizards? In the simplest sense, lizards want to get things right. Many lizards, such as the anoles of the West Indies, live in densely populated areas in which several closely related species may reside. With these species, mating rituals serve as an "ID-check" for prospective suitors. Specifically, when a male approaches a female, questions must be answered. Is the prospective suitor the right species? The right size, color, sex, and age?

Courtship and mating rituals accomplish more than just identification. They also help lizards establish their fitness. For example, fighting among males may sound unnecessary, but the female does have an interest in producing the biggest, strongest, hardiest offspring she can, and mating with the "winner" of a competition may increase the odds for her brood.

Breeding and Courtship

The breeding process operates on a different schedule for each different lizard species. In temperate regions, most species begin courtship in the early spring, so the eggs will hatch by late spring or early summer. This timetable gives newborns as much time as possible to grow in the summer months so that by the time the winter comes, they are mature and robust enough to survive it.

In warmer habitats, breeding may be associated with a rainy or dry season. In every case, mating seems to be timed so that it will give the offspring the maximum chance for survival. Interestingly, one skink, *Eumeces copei*, mates in the fall, just before the animals hibernate. Sperm is stored in the female's body over the winter. When the female awakens in the spring, her eggs are fertilized and the development process begins without delay.

AFTER A TERRITORIAL BATTLE, ONE ANOLE WILL BACK DOWN. THE LOSER WILL SIGNAL HIS DEFEAT WITH A SERIES OF SUBMISSIVE HEAD BOBS.

Most lizard families rely on visual displays for courtship. The anoles of the West Indies are typical of most lizard groups. To initiate courtship, the male anole announces his presence by occupying a conspicuous position. Then the male launches into his display with a series of ritualized flicks, jerks, head bobs, and slow-motion push-ups all designed to show off his colorful dewlap (or other head ornament) to maximum effect, at the same time intimidating rival males and attracting females.

Courtship itself varies with each lizard species. Geckos, for example, are night creatures that do not rely on visual cues for mating behavior. Accordingly, most geckos do not feature colorful crests, dewlaps, body colors, or other visual displays. Instead,

THE ACT OF DEPOSITING SPERM DIRECTLY INSIDE THE FEMALE'S BODY WAS A MAJOR ADVANCE BROUGHT ABOUT BY REPTILES. HERE, THE MALE ANOLE DEPOSITS SPERM INTO THE FEMALE'S ALL-PURPOSE OPENING, THE CLOACA.

they vocalize—squeaking, chirping, and croaking to announce their availability—much more like frogs than other lizards.

If nearby males want to challenge, a scuffle may ensue. Eventually, the victor emerges and gains access to the female. Mating itself can be a rowdy event as the male and female tussle before the male deposits the sperm into the female. Lizard sex organs are different from those of more familiar mammals. Males have a pair of pouchlike organs called hemipenes that are not structurally related to mammalian male sex organs. The female, on the other hand, has no specialized sex organ at all. Sperm is deposited into the cloaca, an all-purpose opening that is used for both excretion and sexual reproduction.

The common side-blotched lizard (a desert iguanid), offers a good example of just how specialized and elaborate mating can be. The males of this species have three different throat colors: blue, orange, and yellow. Each color signifies a different characteristic courtship behavior.

The blue-throated males are guards—they stand by their females and try to fight off intruders. The orange-throated males are intruders—they break into the territory of rival males and try to "steal" mates. The yellow-throated males are sneaks—they get mates by sneaking into the territory of others (sometimes by impersonating females).

One might think that a single throat color would gain an edge over the others in some way. For example, the bold orange-throated intruders might gain mating privileges more often than the other two colors. In fact, this doesn't occur. Any edge that each throat color might gain gets cancelled out by the others in a situation that strongly resembles the children's game, paper-rock-scissors. In the game, outcomes are balanced: paper beats rock, but paper loses to scissors. Similarly, rock beats scissors but loses to paper, and scissors beats paper but loses to rock.

With side-blotched lizards, a similar situation occurs. Blue "guards" are successful in fighting off yellow "sneaks." But the blues cannot fight off the orange "intruders." Meanwhile, the yellow "sneaks" are able to outcompete the orange "intruders," who apparently are not good at guarding.

Male Throat Colors for Side-Blotched Lizards

	beats	loses to
blue	yellow	orange
orange	blue	yellow
yellow	orange	blue

Egg Laying, Development, Birth, and Growth

Reptile development represented a major advance over amphibian development because the reptile embryo formed inside the female's body rather than outside. The number of eggs that a female actually carries, however, and the amount of time that she carries them varies from one lizard family to the next.

Some species lay eggs in an extremely immature state. These relatively undeveloped eggs take a long time to hatch outside the body. Other lizards lay eggs that are quite mature, and they tend to hatch in a much shorter period of time. Still other lizards, such as *Lacerta vivipara*, the common lizard, give birth not to eggs, but to live young.

In fact, five lizard families are viviparous—they give birth to

THESE GILA MONSTER EGGS ARE SOFT AND LEATHERY. LIKE MOST LIZARD EGGS, THEY MUST BE DEPOSITED IN A MOIST PLACE SO THEY WILL NOT DRY OUT. SCIENTISTS SUSPECT THAT GILA MONSTER MATING OCCURS UNDER-GROUND DURING HIBERNATION PERIODS.

live offspring, rather than laying shelled eggs that contain embryos. These are the lacertids, geckos, night lizards, anguids, and skinks. The phenomenon of live birth is generally associated with colder climates. None of the European lacertids, for example, give birth to live young except for *L. vivipara*, which live in the northernmost regions of Europe. Live birth in cool climates makes sense because lizard eggs need a certain amount of warmth to hatch. Though viviparous lizards are ectothermic, the heat they store from their environment makes their bodies considerably warmer than the outside. So keeping eggs inside the body gives them the warmth that they need to hatch successfully, even in cold weather.

The number of eggs that lizards lay also varies from family to family and species to species. The geckos and pygopodids invariably lay only one or two eggs at a time, so they tend to

THE VEILED CHAMELEON TENDS TO BE A SHY AND SOLITARY CREATURE, EXCEPT DURING THE BREEDING SEASON. MALES AND FEMALES ARE ABLE TO TOLERATE EACH OTHERS' PRESENCE ONLY WHEN ACTIVELY COURTING OR MATING.

reproduce more frequently than other families. In other families, clutch size is often much larger and linked to the size of the female itself, with larger females laying a greater number of eggs. The emerald lizard, for example, a lacertid, digs out a 12-inch-long (30.5-cm) tunnel to lay between five and twenty-two eggs at a time. Each egg measures about half an inch (1.3 cm) in length and takes four to twelve weeks to hatch. When lizards hatch, they are fully formed, miniature versions of the adult species. This is another reptile reproductive advance that is not seen in amphibians, which give birth to larval juveniles that must undergo metamorphoses to obtain adult body form.

The most dangerous time in a lizard's life is just after it hatches. At this point, the tiny individual is vulnerable to a host of enemies, including other lizards. Though larger species such as iguanas and monitors can live several decades, most smaller species have a life span of about five to ten years.

Determining Sex

Determining the sex of a lizard is often difficult. To find the sex of a gecko, you must look for a pair of hemipenal bulges on the underside of its body. If the lizard has bulges, it is a male; no bulges means it is a female. Now suppose you did this for a group of one hundred geckos, all of which were hatched under natural conditions at 82.4 degrees Fahrenheit (28° C). How many of them would you guess were female? How many male?

If you said that almost every one of the geckos would be male, and only a handful female—you would be correct! If you looked at a different population that was hatched at a warmer temperature of 89.6 degrees Fahrenheit (32° C), almost all of these would be female!

What is going on here? Can temperature really affect the sex

A FEMALE VEILED CHAMELEON MAY LAY THREE BATCHES OF BETWEEN THIRTY-FIVE
AND EIGHTY-FIVE EGGS PER YEAR.

of a lizard? In fact, the answer to this question is yes for several
lizard families. The phenomenon is called temperature-dependent
sex determination (TSD), and at first glance it appears to violate
fundamental principles of biology. For example, the sex of a rabbit
or a fish or a human being is determined solely by X and Y chromosomes. It does not matter what the temperature is: A fertilized

egg with two X chromosomes produces a female; an egg with an X and a Y chromosome produces a male.

Some lizards, however, don't have sex chromosomes. Instead, their sex is determined by hormones. And these hormones, in turn, are controlled by temperature. Early in development, the hormones travel through the blood to various parts of the body, inducing them to develop male or female characteristics.

Under cold conditions, hormones are secreted to create males. In warm conditions, female-forming hormones are circulated. In conditions that are neither cold nor warm, roughly the same number of males and females develop.

Reproduction without Sex

Some lizards have even stranger ways of reproducing. Imagine looking out over an Arizona landscape with one hundred whiptails running around. All these lizards were born naturally. How many of them are likely to be female?

In this case, the answer is all of them. Lizards of some families can have local populations that are 100 percent female because they reproduce parthenogenically—that is, without sex!

Reproduction without sex—is that possible? Among animals, the process is extremely rare. But plants reproduce asexually all the time. When a cutting is taken from a plant to grow a new plant, sexual reproduction is occurring—or, a clone!

Are the all-female populations of whiptails clones? In fact, they are clones, which brings up a new question: If asexual reproduction is so uncommon, how did it ever arise in such lizard genuses as *Cnemidophorus* in Mexico and the American Southwest and in the lacertid species *Lacerta saxicola* in Europe? In fact, parthenogenesis probably arose when two distinct but similar lizard species mated. When such animal species mate, they often can produce offspring, but those offspring are sterile—that is, the offspring themselves cannot reproduce. An example of this is the mating of a horse and a donkey. It results in a mule, which is sterile and so can't reproduce.

In the case of *Cnemidophorus*, two whiptails of different species probably mated and produced sterile offspring. Somehow those sterile offspring developed a way to start the growth of an egg without its being fertilized by sperm—that is, parthenogenically.

The advantages of this arrangement are significant. Parthenogenic lizards do not need to go through the mating

THE WEB-FOOTED GECKO USES ITS WIDE FEET TO MOVE QUICKLY THROUGH THE SANDS OF ITS HOME IN NAMIBIA, AFRICA. LIKE OTHER GECKOS, THE WEB-FOOTED GECKO REPRODUCES BY LAYING ONLY ONE OR TWO EGGS AT A TIME.

process. They are all female, and they can reproduce without waiting around for the ritual and ceremony that goes along with typical lizard reproduction. Because their generation time is much shorter than that of sexual lizards, parthenogenic lizards can more quickly find a new habitat and take it over.

On the other hand, sex does have its advantages. Parthenogenic lizards are all clones. Every individual is genetically alike. So if there is a change in the environment that threatens a

Unlike other lizard eggs, gecko eggs are typically hard and brittle, much like bird eggs.

population, there is no variety of different genetic types to ensure that some individuals adapt and survive the change. The entire species could be at risk. In this respect, parthenogenic lizards are at a disadvantage.

7 Lizards, Today and Tomorrow

Lizards live all over the world, except for the polar regions, flourishing in almost every kind of habitat. They thrive for a number of reasons. Lizards are hardy—they can survive almost anywhere on almost anything. Most lizard species are insect eaters, relying on prey that is abundant in even the sparsest habitats. Lizards can endure harsh temperatures with little water or food for long periods of time. Because they are ectothermic, lizards can survive on a small fraction of the energy that a similar-sized mammal or bird requires. And lizards are adaptable. The profusion of different kinds of anoles in the West Indies is just one example of how well lizards have been able to adjust to and take over any available habitats.

Nevertheless, lizard habitats are shrinking all over the world. Some lizard species, such as the Gila monster and the Komodo dragon, are officially threatened. It is hard to measure the damage to most other individual species. But all lizards face the

SOME LIZARDS, LIKE THIS TOKAY GECKO, DO NOT SEEM TO BE HARMED BY LAND DEVELOPMENT OR OTHER DISRUPTIVE HUMAN ACTIVITIES.

same general problem. As humans continue to dominate and transform the natural landscape to a greater and greater degree, lizards (and many other species) are being slowly but steadily squeezed out.

Will lizards survive? Most lizard species are in little danger when compared, for example, with their amphibian cousins, the frogs. Since few lizards live in fragile, wet habitats, the forms of pollution and habitat destruction that plague frogs do not pose nearly as great a threat to lizards. Lizards are great survivors; they can often endure extremes that would eliminate even the hardiest mammal, bird, or amphibian. Nevertheless, there is a limit to what lizards can withstand, and that limit may soon be approached as human beings put an ever greater strain on the world's habitats and resources.

Environmental Threats

In general, environmental problems are similar everywhere. People damage ecosystems with air and water pollution, solid-waste and chemical dumping, overuse of pesticides and artificial fertilizers, and large-scale disturbances such as global warming and ozone-layer destruction. These things do untold harm to lizard populations, but their effects are probably dwarfed by the number one human-created problem: land development. As undeveloped areas give way to houses, roads, and factories, lizards and all the other organisms with which they share the ecosystem suffer.

So far, though, it is impossible to tell how badly this hurts lizards. Some lizards, no doubt, are helped by land development and all of the disturbances that come along with it. Geckos seem to thrive in newly developed areas, finding homes in the forest clearings that humans make and in the walls, roofs, and ceilings

PUBLIC OPINION IS IMPORTANT FOR DISCOURAGING THE EXPLOITATION OF REPTILES. IF PEOPLE ACTIVELY DISAPPROVE OF USING REPTILE SKINS TO MAKE BELTS, BOOTS, AND PURSES, SELLERS WILL STOP PUTTING THEM UP FOR SALE.

that they put up. Lacertid wall lizards and rock lizards also seem to benefit from disturbances. They are also abundantly found along walls, open rocky areas, and other artificial habitats.

However, for every lizard genus or group that benefits from human activity, it is reasonable to estimate that there are many species that do not benefit, or are damaged by human interference with natural communities and the food webs that they contain.

Generally, the type of lizard that is threatened in today's world is a specialist of some type, living in a restricted area or feeding on a specialized food source. The type of lizard that tends *not* to be endangered is the generalist—the versatile, wide-ranging species that can thrive in a variety of different habitats and eat a variety of different kinds of prey.

Thus, generalist lizards such as the European wall lizards of the *Podarcis* genus or the *Cnemidophorus* whiptails of North America seem to show no ill effects from environmental disturbances. Equally at home in a variety of habitats—rocks, grasses, desert, and so on—these lizards are flexible enough to survive and even thrive in ecosystems that have been compromised in some way.

The types of lizard that do end up being threatened or endangered are the specialists. These include monitor lizards, such as the Komodo dragon, the Galapagos marine iguana, and many chameleon species that live in specialized, restricted areas. Many island lizards, such as the sail-fin lizard or the Culebra Island giant anole are also on the endangered or vulnerable lists. Island ecosystems are known to be much more fragile than those on the mainland, so island lizards feel the "squeeze" more readily than do their mainland counterparts.

A classic case of a threatened specialist is the California horned toads of the genus *Phrynosoma*. These creatures traditionally feed on a species of large ants that are native to their California habitat. About one hundred years ago, a new species of smaller, more aggressive ants was introduced to the area from Argentina, probably arriving as stowaways aboard a ship. This new ant species started to take over the niche of the ants that the horned toads prefer. Still, there was no real problem until very recently, when land development, in the form of nearby building projects, suddenly disturbed local ecosystems and accelerated the advance of the Argentine ants into new habitats.

Suddenly things have changed. The old, "tasty" ants are largely gone. The smaller Argentine ants have replaced them.

As a result, the survival of the horned toads is now threatened because they are unable to find their favorite prey, and they refuse to eat the smaller Argentine ants. It is easy to see how disturbances like these can echo their way throughout an entire ecosystem. If horned toads begin to disappear, the predators that rely on them may also be harmed, and the predators that eat those predators presumably will also suffer. One can only guess just how many situations like this one an ecosystem can take before its food-web relationships begin to unravel completely.

Human Threats

Direct threats to lizards that are not a result of environmental degradation fall into three basic categories. First, there is what can only be described as ignorance or mistaken identity. For example, in Australia many blue-tongued skinks were killed because people mistakenly thought they were venomous. (The heloderms of North America are the world's only venomous lizards.) In Africa, chameleons were killed for the same reason. Snake lizards are still routinely mistaken for snakes and destroyed out of the general fear of snakes that many people have.

Another traditional danger for lizards is hunting. While hunting lizards is on the decline, larger lizards such as the iguana are still sought as food sources. Similarly, a number of large lizard species, including iguanas and monitors, are hunted for their skins in order to make elegant boots, gloves, handbags, and other items. The best way to combat this form of exploitation is through public disapproval. As with fur coats, if people refuse to buy lizard-skin products, the market for lizard skins will dry up.

The pet trade is perhaps the greatest nonenvironmental problem for lizards. As many as 2 million iguanas are imported into the United States each year, but this represents only a fraction of the number of animals that are actually captured for export. In a typical capture sequence, the ingenuity of iguanas is actually used against them. Normally iguanas can escape predators by leaping from the high branch of a tree to safety below. Human predators take advantage of this escape strategy by employing two-person hunting teams. One hunter chases the iguana up the tree. The other hunter waits below, capturing the animal in a net as it jumps to what appears to be safety.

Each year a number of other lizard species are brought to the pet market around the world, only a portion of which survive for more than a few months. Other than iguanas, the most popular lizard pets include leopard and tokay geckos, blue-tongued skinks, several anole species, bearded dragons, water dragons, *Uromastyx* dabb lizards, sungazers, chameleons, and savanna monitors.

Perhaps the greatest overall threat to lizards is their general hardiness. Lizards are able to withstand almost any kind of hardship. Unlike mammals or birds, most lizards can easily go for a month or more without food. They can also withstand extremes of temperature and lack of moisture much better than many other creatures.

Pet traders prey on this hardiness, confining lizards to inhospitable places for long periods of time, confident that these robust creatures can endure even the most extreme conditions. The result is that many lizards end up losing their lives due to neglect and mistreatment.

In their natural environment, a similar peril exists for lizards. Because of their ability to withstand extremes, many lizard species are not visibly harmed by pollution, habitat loss, and other threats of human origin that endanger other animal groups such as amphibians, birds, and mammals. This does not

CAN A LIZARD, LIKE THIS SAND LIZARD, BE LOVABLE? GO ASK SOMEONE WHO HAS SPENT TIME WITH A LIZARD.

mean that sooner or later these creatures, along with their more vulnerable relatives, will not suffer the consequences of environmental degradation.

Glossary

adaptation—a change in body form or function as a result of natural selection

amniotic egg—an egg that includes a water-containing membrane that surrounds the embryo

amphibians—the first land animals

anapsids—animals with no skull holes

camouflage—coloring and body pattern that helps hide an animal in plain sight

chromatophores—special pigment cells

chromosomes—cell structures that contain DNA and instructions for development of the cell into an organism

cloaca—all-purpose body opening for reproduction and elimination

clutch—number of eggs laid at one time

courtship behavior—behavior that is used to gain favor with the opposite sex for mating

crocodilian—an animal whose legs are tucked part of the way under its body

dewlap—flap of skin under the chin

diapsids—animals with two skull holes; the diapsid line split into two branches, which led to dinosaurs, birds, and modern reptiles

display—showing off colors, posing, and preening in order to gain the favor of the opposite sex for mating

DNA—deoxyribonucleic acid, the substance inside every cell that contains the genetic code; DNA is used to determine how closely different animal species are related

ecosystem—physical and biological parts of an organism's environment

ectotherm—cold-blooded animal that relies mainly on its environment for heat

egg—female reproductive cell that combines with sperm to form a new organism

embryo—immature form of animal that has not been hatched or born

endotherm—warm-blooded animal that generates its own body heat

frill—head ornament on several lizard species, especially iguanids and agamids

habitat—the environment in which an animal species lives

hemipene—paired male sex organ

hormones—chemical released by glands that travel through the blood and affect the body systems

iguanian—a member of the lizard group that includes the iguanids, the agamids, and the chameleons

internal fertilization—uniting of egg and sperm inside the body of the female

Jacobsen's organ—a sensory organ in the roof of the mouth that performs a function similar to the sense of smell

melatonin—a hormone that regulates a lizard's night-day cycles

metabolism—the speed at which an organism's "engine" runs

natural selection—the process of selecting for traits that increase the chances of an animal's survival

nocturnal—active during the night

oxygen—atmospheric gas that all animals use to burn their food to get energy

parthenogenesis—reproduction without sex; occurs when the egg begins dividing without joining sperm

pigment—color material

pineal gland—a lizard's "third eye"; it controls light-dark cycles for metabolism

population—the number of animals of a given species in a given place

predator—animal that seeks other animals for food

prehensile—a limb that can grasp

prey—animal that is hunted for food by a predator

reptile—four-legged land vertebrae with scales; it is ectothermic and usually lays eggs: snakes, lizards, turtles, crocodilians, and tuataras

species—organism that is distinctly different from other types and generally reproduces only with its own kind

sperm—male reproductive cell that combines with an egg to form a new organism

sprawl—degree to which legs are tucked underneath the body

Squamata—order of reptiles that includes lizards and snakes

synapsid—animals with one skull hole; an evolutionary line that led to mammal-like reptiles and later led to mammals themselves

territoriality—behavior of animals that fight over space, usually for mating rights

temperature-dependent sex determination—animals in which the sex of their offspring is largely determined by the temperature of their hatching environment

vertebrate—animals with backbones, including fish, amphibians, reptiles, birds, and mammals

viviparous—animals that give birth to live young

zygodactylous—toe arrangement in which two toes point inward and the other three point outward

yolk—food source in an amniotic egg

Species Checklist

Region	Number of Lizard Families	Common Families	Unique to this Region
North America (to Mexico)	8	Teiid race runners Skinks	Heloderms (Gila monster)
Central and South America	5	Iguanids of all types Skinks Small geckos	
Northern Europe, Asia, Africa	6	Wall lizards (lacertids) in Europe Agamids in Africa	
Southern Africa	7	Agamids Skinks Geckos Chameleons Monitors	Girdled lizards
China, India, Southeast Asia	10	Agamids Geckos Lacertids Skinks Anguids Monitors	Blind worms Earless monitor
Australia	4	Geckos Agamids Skinks Monitors	

Evolutionary Timetable

NOTE: mya=millions of years ago

Periods	Events
Before 600 mya: **Precambrian**	
500–600 mya: **Cambrian**	
440–500 mya: **Ordivician**	**500** mya: Life first appears on land
400–440 mya: **Silurian**	**400** mya: First land animals (arthropods)
345–400 mya: **Devonian**	**350** mya: Amphibians first appear
290–345 mya: **Carboniferous**	**315** mya: Reptiles first appear
	290 mya: First great reptile expansion
245–290 mya: **Permian**	**270** mya: Turtlelike animals appear
195–245 mya: **Triassic**	**210** mya: Dawn of dinosaurs; Second great reptile expansion began
	200 mya: First lizard appears, *Prolacterta*
	195 mya: Doglike reptiles that go on to become mammals appear
138–195 mya: **Jurassic**	**170** mya: Flying reptiles appear
66–138 mya: **Cretaceous**	**100** mya: Snakes appear
2–66 mya: **Tertiary**	**65** mya: Great extinction: End of dinosaurs and the Age of Reptiles
0–2 mya: **Quarternary**	

Further Research

Books for Young People

Bartlett, Richard D., and Patricia Pope Bartlett. *A–Z of Lizard Care*. New York: Barrons Educational Series, 1997.

Cherry, Jim. *Loco for Lizards*. Northland, AZ: Northland Publishers, 2000.

Kaplan, Melissa. *Iguanas for Dummies*. New York: John Wiley and Sons, 2000.

Mattison, Chris. *Keeping and Breeding Lizards*. Pittsburgh: Blandford Press, 1991.

McCarthy, Colin. *Reptile*. New York: Dorling-Kindersley, 1991.

Schneiper, Claudia. *Lizards*. Minneapolis, MN: Carolrhoda Books, 1988.

Web Sites

There are dozens of lizard sites on the Internet. Here are some good ones.

http://reptilehunter3520.tripod.com/thereptilehunterslair

http://www.reptileassociation.com/index.html

http://animal.discovery.com/guides/atoz/snakes.html

http://www.reptiletopsites.com/cgi-bin/eng/topsites/lizards/topsites.html

http://www.embl-heidelberg.de/~uetz/LivingReptiles.html

http://www.nafcon.dircon.co.uk/index_mag_lizards.html

http://www.animaldiversity.ummz.umich.edu/index.html

http://www.desertusa.com/reptiles/reptiles_ab1.html

Bibliography

Bartlett, Richard. D., and Patricia Pope Bartlett. *Anoles*. New York: Barrons Educational Series, 2001.

Beheler, John. *Reptiles and Amphibians of the World*. New York: Simon & Schuster, 1989.

Fox, Stanley F. *Lizard Social Behavior*. Baltimore, MD: Johns Hopkins University Press, 2003.

Halliday, Tim, and Adler Kraig, eds. *The Encyclopedia of Reptiles and Amphibians*. New York: Facts on File, 1986.

"How Geckos Get a Grip," *Scientific American News*, August 27, 2002.

Losos, Jonathan B. "A Lizard's Tale," *Scientific American*, March 2001.

Martin, James. "The Engaging Habits of Chameleons Suggest Mirth More than Menace," *Smithsonian*, 1990, 21:44-53.

Mattison, Chris. *Lizards of the World*. Pittsburgh: Blandford Press, 1999.

Steel, Rodney. *Living Dragons*. Pittsburgh: Blandford Press, 1998.

Index

Page numbers in **boldface** are illustrations.

About the Author

DAN GREENBERG is the author of *Whales* and *Dolphins*, two other books in our AnimalWays series. He has also written on a variety of other topics, including spiders, chimpanzees, roller coasters, baseball, frogs, and U.S. history. There are now more than twelve titles in his series of best-selling educational books, including *Comic Book Math* and *Comic Book Grammar*. Greenberg lives in Westchester County, New York, with his wife, two children, and a beagle.